COCKPITS
OF THE COLD WAR

In memory of the pilots and aircrew who gave their lives
while serving their countries during the Cold War.

COCKPITS
OF THE COLD WAR

BY DONALD NIJBOER

WITH PHOTOGRAPHS BY DAN PATTERSON
FOREWORD BY AIR VICE-MARSHAL RON DICK, RAF (RET.)

A BOSTON MILLS PRESS BOOK

National Library of Canada Cataloging in Publication
Nijboer, Donald, 1959-
    Cockpits of the cold war / Donald Nijboer ; with
photographs by Dan Patterson ; foreword by Ron Dick.

Includes bibliographical references and index.
ISBN 1-55046-405-1

1. Airplanes, Military — Cockpits.   2. Airplanes,
Military — History. I. Patterson, Dan, 1953— II. Title.

TL681.C6N543 2003   623.7' 46049   C2003-901181-X

07 06 05 04 03   1 2 3 4 5

Publisher Cataloging-in-Publication Data   (U.S.)
Nijboer, Donald, 1959-
    Cockpits of the cold war / Donald Nijboer ; with
photographs by Dan Patterson ; foreword by Ron Dick.
— 1st ed.
[ ] p. : col. ill. , photos. ; cm.
Includes bibliographical references and index.
Summary: A history and detailed description of the
cockpits from 1950's and 1960's military aircraft,
each from a pilot's perspective.

ISBN 1-55046-405-1
1. Airplanes, Military — Cockpits.   2. Airplanes,
Military — History. I. Patterson, Dan, 1953— II. Title.

623.7/ 46049 21   TL681.C6N543 2003

Published by BOSTON MILLS PRESS
132 Main Street,
Erin, Ontario N0B 1T0
Tel 519-833-2407
Fax 519-833-2195
books@bostonmillspress.com
www.bostonmillspress.com

IN CANADA:
Distributed by Firefly Books Ltd.
3680 Victoria Park Avenue
Toronto, Ontario M2H 3K1

IN THE UNITED STATES:
Distributed by Firefly Books (U.S.) Inc.
P.O. Box 1338, Ellicott Station
Buffalo, New York 14205

Design: PageWave Graphics
Printed in Singapore

The publisher acknowledges the financial support
of the Government of Canada through the Book
Publishing Industry Development Program (BPIDP)
for its publishing efforts.

Cover: A parked Javelin of No. 33 Squadron RAF,
Bruggen, Germany, 1959. The Gloster Javelin was built
as a replacement for the Meteor nightfighter in the
all-weather interceptor role.
Cover Inset: F-86A Sabre cockpit.

Half Title Page: The Saab J 32 Lansen was very a popular
aircraft, much liked by its pilots. Although neutral during
the Cold War, the Swedish Air Force modeled their unit
structure and tactics on their Western counterparts.

Title Page: A pressure-suited SR-71 pilot ready for take-off.
Able to operate at Mach 3 in the upper atmosphere, the
SR-71 had a radar return far smaller than most modern
jet fighters of today.

Opposite: The futuristic looking F-104 was tailor-made for
the air superiority bomber-interceptor role. While extremely
fast, the early F-104 suffered from a notoriously short range.

Opposite Contents Page: A Valiant crew run to their aircraft
during a Quick Reaction Alert (QRA) practice exercise.

CONTENTS

FOREWORD

The coming of the Cold War saw the coming of the jets. With the advent of turbine power, the world of aviation changed dramatically and forever. Seen from the cockpit, perhaps the most disturbing effect was the disappearance of the propeller. Experienced aviators, seasoned by endless hours behind the pistons of World War II, often found the absence of a reassuring whirling disc unsettling. The thin whining of the new engines was no substitute for the earthy, heart-warming roar of powerful reciprocating machinery. However, in the early days of the jet revolution, the majority of pilots who formed the first-generation jet squadrons had very little experience of any kind. Most of them were straight from training on piston-engined aircraft such as the T6 Texan (the Harvard in the RAF), and for them, the transition to the kerosene-breathing monsters was a challenging business — exhilarating, demanding and, on occasion, frightening. There were things about jet aircraft cockpits, in particular, that seemed a little strange to both the neophyte and the old and bold.

During WWII, the cockpits of military aircraft had developed to some degree, but for the most part the basic arrangements had remained comfortably familiar. From the point of view of his immediate surroundings, the pilot of a Spitfire in the Battle of Britain would have found, four years later, few surprises lurking in the cockpit of a Typhoon or P-51 Mustang. In early jet aircraft such as the Gloster Meteor, the Lockheed P-80 or the MiG-9, however, significant changes began to appear. The most obvious were instantly apparent — levels of noise and vibration were sharply reduced, and, for single-engined fighter pilots especially, fields of vision were wonderfully improved. Inside the cockpit, the engine instruments were different, indicating novel details such as jet-pipe temperature and allowing for seemingly astronomical engine rpm. The basic flight instruments, too, seemed intent on exaggeration, showing speeds and rates of climb that were hard to accept, as was the pace at which the fuel-gauge needles raced across their dials toward zero. Air brakes (speed brakes in the United States) were standard fittings, as were relight systems, since shut-down engines had to be painstakingly relit rather than rapidly unfeathered.

Meteor F.8s going through their aerobatic paces. No. 64 Squadron formed the RAF Aerobatic team from 1953 until 1954.

Increases in operating heights and speeds were exciting advances, but they trailed problems in their wake. More attention had to be paid to the effects such developments had on the aircrew. Pressurized cockpits became the norm rather than the exception, and ejection seats were introduced to allow high-speed escapes from doomed aircraft. High speed also forced the introduction of powered flying controls to ease the pain of heavy stick forces. Such things as G-suits, protective helmets ("bone domes"), and flame-resistant clothing followed, and designers slowly became conscious of the need to listen to aircrew opinions and to think seriously about a sadly neglected subject — cockpit ergonomics.

From the 1950s onward, as aircraft performance continued to improve, aircraft systems kept pace by becoming more complex. Multi-role aircraft exacerbated the situation. Aircrew workloads increased accordingly, but little thought was given initially to ensuring that the "man/machine interface" was efficiently designed.

Accidents were frequent and most were attributed to pilot error. Despite the haphazard arrangement of instruments and controls so evident in early military jet aircraft cockpits, the possibility that the way information was being presented to the pilot might be a contributing factor in many accidents was seldom, if ever, considered. Decades passed before it was fully accepted that designers had to ensure that aircrew were kept aware at all times of what was happening (and what was likely to happen) both inside and outside the cockpit, that the equipment carrying the necessary data was logically arranged, and that information was made available to aircrew in a way that allowed sensible, rapid decisions to be made.

As the Cold War dragged on, a new word entered the dictionary — avionics. It was an umbrella term used to cover an aircraft's navigation, communications, flight data and control systems. Interconnected and integrated within the compact space of a combat aircraft's cockpit, these systems are a mix of computers, sensors, actuators, and control and display units. Most information is displayed in color on flat CRT screens instead of being spread over an ill-assorted collection of clock faces. HUDs (Head Up Displays) allow pilots to keep their heads up and eyes out while flying at high speed and low level, or while approaching to land in bad weather. These and other systems helped to revolutionize the way combat aircraft cockpits are designed and used. Among the innovations were moving map displays, HOTAS (Hands On Throttle And Stick), FLIR (Forward Looking Infra-Red), and night-vision goggles. The F-16 added an ejection seat inclined at 30 degrees and a side-stick controller. Much of the routine business of managing aircraft systems and detecting system failures now became the responsibility of the on-board computers, allowing the pilot to take his or her place as an integral part of the human/computer/airframe weapons system and to concentrate on seeing that the machine did its job in combat.

Having gained my RAF wings in the Harvard, and having survived flying some of the early jets in the 1950s, I experienced many of the cockpit changes introduced during the Cold War. In 1988, I took my last flight in a front-line military aircraft. It was an F-16. Any resemblance between the cockpit of the F-16 and that of the Meteor I had flown thirty-six years before seemed coincidental. Looking back over my career, I had to confess that my gray hair was showing and that, if I were honest, I was more at home in less sophisticated surroundings. The young squadron pilots who flew the F-16 operationally had been brought up with computers and took to modern cockpits naturally. I admired their remarkable professionalism and proficiency, but for my part I rather resented needing artificial intelligence to fly the aircraft and felt that, instead of being master of the machine, I appeared to have become merely an element in an integrated weapons system. The F-16 deflated my ego and made me realize just how much military cockpits (and pilots) had changed since WWII. As the illustrations in this book clearly show, those changes have been considerable. Some things, however, never change, and the suggestion I made in the foreword to the first book in Donald Nijboer's revealing series still seems apt: The term "cockpit" defines the place where aviation's fighting cocks face their challenges and fight their battles.

AVM Ron Dick, Virginia, January 2003

PHOTOGRAPHER'S PREFACE

When I was a little kid, my fascination with airplanes and machines that went really fast and made a lot of great noise was taking shape. I grew up in Dayton, Ohio, where aviation got its start and where there was (and still is) a large Air Force base nearby. My mom and dad will tell you that whenever the sounds of an airplane drifted through the windows, I was out the door and looking to the sky to see what possibly might be flying overhead. The nearby base often brought the newest, biggest and loudest airplanes in the inventory. One of my favorite rides in the car was to the local airport to watch the "planes."

Funny — now that I am in my fiftieth year, I still act that way, and often find myself driving past the airport just to see what's around.

Many of the subjects of this book, the military jets of the Cold War, were what I wanted to see. Those were the hottest and the fastest and the coolest flying machines around. Air shows brought them a little closer and made them all that much more "real." My friend Paul Perkins and I used to live for the spring air show at the airbase and would plan for

weeks our excursion from downtown Dayton out to the airbase, catching the bus at the terminal at the earliest possible time to be sure to get to the gate when it opened. We had to be there first. We were rarely disappointed. I distinctly recall the year we got there at the crack of dawn and found that the RAF had sent one of their very exotic looking Handley Page Victor bombers to the show. We were used to seeing B-52 bombers, but this looked like something from another planet.

The latest and greatest was never available to see close up. The SR-71 Blackbird was flown by at a distance, but never close enough to "see." We read the British aviation magazines and wondered what the English Electric "Lightning" was like, and Russian airplanes… well, good luck. "We'll never, ever get to see one of those."

Dreams do come true. The little kid in me is smiling. What were once the most top secret and classified state-of-the-art military jets are now museum pieces. Aviation museums in four countries on both sides of the Atlantic have provided access to the Cold War jets of five nations, including the RAF Victor, the Lightning, the SR-71 and many Russian jets.

Our previous book, *Cockpit: An Illustrated History of World War II Aircraft Interiors*, provided a look into the flying experiences of the pilots and a glimpse into the evolutionary development of the airplane. This book continues that process. While the number of gauges and switches has increased and the complexity of the systems has expanded, the basics of flying are still in front of the pilot. A "Cold Warrior" told me that when all was going wrong and the expanded systems and extra switches were made useless due to a failure, the basics — the compass, the turn-and-bank indicator and the altimeter, along with the stick and rudder — and flying by the seat of your pants would, in fact, get you home.

Dan Patterson,
Dayton, Ohio, April 2003

INTRODUCTION

The Cold War will probably go down in history as the longest non-shooting war (between the major powers) in the history of mankind. At the end of the Second World War, Eastern Europe was firmly in the grips of the Communists. The vast Russian army that destroyed the bulk of the German army in the East was looked upon by those in the West as a direct threat. In response, the North Atlantic Treaty Organization (NATO) was formed in 1949. With direct support from the United States, countries such as Britain, France, Holland, Denmark, Germany, Norway and others were able to build up their armed forces and, in particular, they were able to acquire new jet fighters.

First-generation fighters such as the Meteor, Sea Hawk, F-84 and CF-100 were almost twice as fast as their propeller predecessors — and they had to be. The introduction of the jet engine and the nuclear bomb changed the military landscape forever. The threat of nuclear holocaust was now very real. The new interceptors had to be able to get airborne as quickly as possible, find their target and shoot it down. New bombers were also being developed, all designed to carry a large nuclear device with a range of at least 3,500 miles! The race was on. The number of new jet aircraft designed and built in the 1950s was staggering. Production rates, while not as high as in World War II, were considerable. So rapid was the advancement in aerodynamics and engine development that some types, the F11 Tiger and Supermarine Scimitar, for instance, saw only a few years of service, while others such as the MiG-21 and B-52 continue to fly to this day. But there was a dark side. The new jet aircraft were the first of their kind, and accident rates were staggering. Pilots did not have the luxury of training on flight simulators before their first flight. In most cases it was a matter of here's the book, there's the plane. Pilots were also experiencing new and strange flight characteristics never encountered before. In some cases they had to fly their aircraft on missions for which they were not designed.

Through Dan Patterson's amazing photographs we get to see, up close, the cockpits that were on the front line of the Cold War. The evolution of the jet cockpit is clearly revealed, from the Gloster Meteor and F-80 to the once top-secret SR-71 and still operational MiG-21. Congressman Randy Cunningham, Brigadier General Robin Olds, Colonel Bud Mahurin, Colonel Bud Anderson, George Day and Byron Hukee are among the combat pilots who provide their insights and thoughts on what it was like to fly and fight in some of the cockpits featured in this book. We also hear from those pilots and test pilots who never fired a shot — those who stood on nuclear alert, endured countless hours on patrol, or were catapulted from a carrier flight deck on the North Atlantic day after day, night after night.

The design, development and construction of jet combat aircraft during the 1950s and 1960s has no match in any other period in aviation history, and the incredible advances of that time will never be repeated. *Cockpits of the Cold War* gives us a close-up glimpse of what it must have been like to fly in some of the most feared and revered aircraft ever built.

Donald Nijboer,
Toronto, Canada, March 2003

"Grady moved the yoke and the Vindicator leveled off. The slight strain on his harness relaxed. He glanced around his limited arc of sky and saw it turning from a crystal gray to a deep endless blue. Then he received two signals which made his body go rigid even before his mind understood fully what had happened. In his earphones there was a sudden beeping noise repeated in short staccato bursts. Automatically he looked down at the Fail-Safe box which was installed between him and the bombardier. For the first time in his flying career the bulb on the top of the box was glowing red. Then his intellect caught up with his reflexes: this was the real thing. Both he and Thomas looked up from the Fail-Safe box simultaneously. Thomas's eyes seemed nonchalant. Grady's response was unhesitating. He reached for the S.S.B radio switch. This would put him in direct contact with Omaha. It was the positive Control double check. Immediately, Grady knew, he would hear from Omaha the reassuring 'No go.' Something had gone wrong with the Fail-Safe box. It would be all corrected. He flipped on the S.S.B. switch. A loud, pulsating drone filled his ears. No voice signal was possible."

Eugene Burdick and Harvey Wheeler,
Fail Safe, *Dell Publishing, 1962*

Left: A Polish Air Force MiG-21MF.

CANADA

AVRO CF-100

AVRO

CF-100

NICKNAMED THE CLUNK, THE LEAD SLED, THE ZILCH — THE CF-100 PROVED
TO BE THE BEST FIRST-GENERATION ALL-WEATHER JET FIGHTER OF THE COLD WAR
AND THE ONLY CANADIAN-DESIGNED FIGHTER TO GO INTO MASS PRODUCTION

As World War II drew to a close, the aircraft industry in Canada was at an all-time high. In June 1945, Victory Aircraft, which built Lancasters at its Malton plant, became Avro Canada. In August 1949, looking for markets for advanced aircraft, the young company produced the Avro Canada C-102 Jetliner. It was a successful aircraft, but the C-102 was a product ahead of its time. The market for short-haul jetliners simply didn't exist. Earlier, in 1946, the Royal Canadian Air Force had realized the need for an all-weather fighter to defend the huge expanse of Canada. After talking with the Americans and British for a possible solution, the Canadians decided to write their own specification. The challenge the RCAF had put forward was astonishing. It was like asking for an aircraft with the range of Fw 200 Condor, the climb of a Bachem Ba 349 Natter, and the speed of an Me 262. The new fighter was to have a crew of two, advanced all-weather radar, heavy gun armament and a combination of speed, rate of climb and range never seen before.

While there were many new jet engines available in the United States and Great Britain, Avro Canada had made the decision to push ahead once again with its own design. As Avro Canada moved ahead with the CF-100 airframe, it was decided to use the Rolls-Royce AJ.65 Avon jet engine to power the prototype. But the Gas Turbine Division of Avro Canada had been working on a new engine during the war, and in 1948, manufacture of the engine prototype got underway. It was nicely timed for the CF-100. Test runs of the first Orenda engine were a great success and, although the British Avon and Sapphire engines were just as good, the new engine was Canadian and that meant a lot.

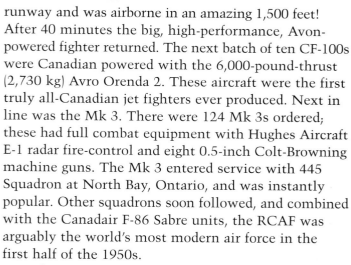

On January 19, 1950, the first CF-100 took to the skies. The all-black fighter, light on fuel, streaked down the runway and was airborne in an amazing 1,500 feet! After 40 minutes the big, high-performance, Avon-powered fighter returned. The next batch of ten CF-100s were Canadian powered with the 6,000-pound-thrust (2,730 kg) Avro Orenda 2. These aircraft were the first truly all-Canadian jet fighters ever produced. Next in line was the Mk 3. There were 124 Mk 3s ordered; these had full combat equipment with Hughes Aircraft E-1 radar fire-control and eight 0.5-inch Colt-Browning machine guns. The Mk 3 entered service with 445 Squadron at North Bay, Ontario, and was instantly popular. Other squadrons soon followed, and combined with the Canadair F-86 Sabre units, the RCAF was arguably the world's most modern air force in the first half of the 1950s.

In the United States, the USAF was moving toward all-rocket armament for their all-weather interceptors. The RCAF followed suit, and the new Mk 4 was equipped with the advanced "collision course" fire-control radar and wingtip pods each housing 29 or 30 Mighty Mouse rockets. A total of 510 Mk 4s were produced and served from 1953 to 1959. The last version of the CF-100 to see service was the Mk 5. In 1956, the RCAF brought the CF-100 to Europe. There they served in the much-needed all-weather defense of NATO.

With over 30 years of service, the CF-100 proved to be one of the most rugged, reliable and versatile all-weather fighters ever produced. In the end, over 692 were built.

Left: A brace of CF-100 Mk 4Bs in 423 Squadron colors. The main armament of the Mk 4 was the 2.75-inch unguided rocket and a ventral gun pack housing eight .50-caliber machine guns. Above: The CF-100 Mk 5 was the last version to see service with the RCAF. Improvements to the aircraft included wingtip and horizontal tail extensions and the absence of a gun bay.

PILOT'S PERSPECTIVE
Major Don Gregory
RCAF (Ret.)

The first CF-100 I climbed into was a Mk 3. That was a real mess. The stick was offset 11 degrees so you could see the compass, which was set low on the instrument panel.

The Mk 5 cockpit was pretty good. Generally speaking, things were reasonably placed and there wasn't too much cross-hand stuff, except when you had to connect the auto-pilot, which was on the right-hand side. The Mk 5 was one of the first airplanes where they actually started to think a little about where they put the instruments.

The "Clunk" was my first operational aircraft. Compared to the T-Bird cockpit, the CF-100's was actually a little tighter. The T-Bird had a wider cockpit with more canopy. Instrument layouts were fairly similar. Engine instruments were on the right and easy to read. The side-by-side vertical arrangement only required a glance to see what was going on. Most of the critical stuff was in a reasonable position. The comfort level in the cockpit on a scale of 1 to 10 was about a 4 or 5.

Visibility was all right. The workload in the CF-100 was not extreme. It was an easy airplane to fly, and very stable, so it was good to fly on instruments. Most of our flying was at night and in bad weather.

You didn't want to fly the CF-100 without hydraulics. Because it was an articulated stick in the left-right mode, you needed two hands to make a left turn without hydraulics. It was very heavy. In pitch it wasn't so bad, because you had the whole length of the stick as a lever.

If I could change anything in the CF-100, it would have been the heater. That was the coldest airplane I have ever flown. The heater inlet was located on the rear right fuselage. From there the outside air was mixed with the hot air generated by the engines and then passed forward through about 25 feet of unheated, unpressurized fuselage. By the time it reached my feet, it was stone cold again. Whenever we flew, heating controls were on full, even in summer.

AVRO CF-100 MK 4
Imperial War Museum, Duxford, England

1. Canopy Declutch Pull Handle
2. Engine Throttle Lever
3. Oxygen Cylinder Pressure Gauge
4. Elevator Trim Position Indicator
5. Landing Flap Position Indicator
6. Gunsight Dimmer Switch
7. Gunsight
8. Fire Warning Light / Engine Extinguisher
9. Rudder Pedal Control
10. Landing Gear Position Indicator
11. Landing Gear Warning Light
12. Emergency and Parking Brake Lever
13. Radio Channel Indicator Switch
14. Airspeed Indicator
15. Machmeter
16. Hydraulic Pressure Gauge
17. Guns Holdback Release Switch
18. Rudder Pedal
19. Auto Trim Warning Light
20. Fusilage Tank Low Level Warning Light RH
21. Fusilage Tank Low Level Warning Light RH
22. Generator Warning Light
23. Generator Warning Light
24. Gyro Erection Push Button Switch
25. Gyro Compass
26. Rate-of-Climb Indicator
27. Gunsight Gauging Button
28. Control Column
29. Bombs and Rockets Firing Button
30. Elevator Trim Switch
31. Attitude Gyro Indicator
32. Pilot's Flight Indicator
33. Fire Warning Light RH Engine
34. Wing Tank Fuel Press Warning Light LH
35. Wing Tank Fuel Press Warning Light RH
36. Engine Fuel Press Warning Light LH
37. Engine Fuel Press Warning Light RH
38. Radio Compass
39. Altimeter
40. RPM Indicator
41. Emergency Inverter Warning Light
42. RPM Indicator
43. Exhaust Temp Gauges
44. Fuel Quantity Gauges
45. Oil Pressure Gauges
46. Bomb Arming Switch
47. Bomb-Rocket Selector Switch

Two members of 440 Squadron are seen climbing into the cockpit of their Mk 4 CF-100 in its standard NATO camouflage colors.

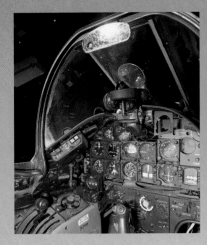

DOUGLAS
A-1 SKYRAIDER

LOCKHEED F-80
SHOOTING STAR

REPUBLIC F-84
THUNDERJET

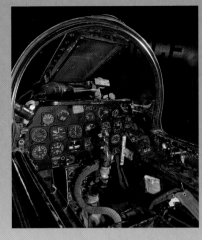

NORTH AMERICAN
F-86 SABRE

McDONNELL
F-101 VOODOO

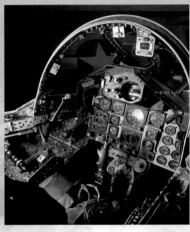

McDONNELL
F-4 PHANTOM

LOCKHEED
F-104 STARFIGHTER

REPUBLIC F-105
THUNDERCHIEF

CONVAIR
F-106 DELTA DART

LOCKHEED
SR-71 BLACKBIRD

CONVAIR
B-36 PEACEMAKER

GRUMMAN F9F
PANTHER/COUGAR

UNITED STATES OF AMERICA

NORTH AMERICAN
F-100 SUPER SABRE

BOEING B-47 STRATOJET

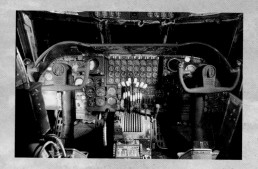

BOEING B-52
STRATOFORTRESS

VOUGHT
F8 CRUSADER

DOUGLAS
F4D SKYRAY

GRUMMAN
F11 TIGER

DOUGLAS

A-1 SKYRAIDER

THE PROPELLER-DRIVEN SKYRAIDER WAS ONE OF THE MOST REMARKABLE AIRCRAFT OF
THE COLD WAR. IT SAW SERVICE IN TWO WARS AND WAS REGARDED BY MANY
AS THE MOST EFFECTIVE GROUND-ATTACK AIRCRAFT EVER BUILT.

With the lessons of the Pacific war well in hand, the U.S. Navy began looking for a replacement for the venerable SBD Dauntless. The new "Dauntless II," as it was called, was designed around one of the most powerful piston engines ever built, the Wright R-3350-24 powerplant, rated at 2,500 horsepower. Armed with two 20 mm cannon in each wing and three bomb racks on each wing and one on the fuselage centerline, the XBT2D-1 prototype flew for the first time on March 18, 1945. One month later, on May 5, 1945, the Navy ordered 598 Dauntless IIs, but this was cut back to 277 after VJ Day. In February 1946, the Dauntless II was renamed the AD-1 (nicknamed Able Dog) Skyraider and, in late 1947, was deployed aboard the U.S.S *Midway*. The Skyraider quickly showed its versatility. The new aircraft was soon modified to fly as an airborne early warning aircraft, night attack aircraft, reconnaissance and electronic countermeasures vehicle.

When the North Koreans crossed the 38th Parallel in June 1950, production of the Skyraider was being phased out in order to make room for more advanced jet attack aircraft. However, during subsequent operations, the Skyraider showed it could do more than the new jet fighters built to replace it. The Skyraider's ability to lift up to 8,000 pounds (3,630 kg) of ordnance and stay on station for hours at a time made it an ideal close-support aircraft, and no jet fighter anywhere could match its performance! The lessons of the Korean War would carry the Skyraider well into the Vietnam War. When America entered the war, ten U.S. Navy and Marine attack squadrons were still equipped with the piston-engine bomber. During the war, Skyraider squadrons were credited with no

fewer than twenty-nine Yankee Station cruises in the Gulf of Tonkin. Navy and Marine service for the Skyraider ended in 1968, but the aircraft would serve even longer with the U.S Air Force. In mid-1962 the U.S. Air Force evaluated the Skyraider and, as a result, sent 75 A-1E Skyraiders to Vietnam. In the beginning, U.S. Air Force experience with the Skyraider was limited to the side-by-side version of the A-1E. But as the single-seat versions, A-1H and A-1Js, began leaving the Navy inventory in 1967, the Air Force gobbled them up. All told, the U.S. Air Force would use 450 Skyraiders, and during the peak years of 1969 and 1970, there were more than 100 Skyraiders in four Special Operations Squadrons.

The Skyraider was ideal for the missions assigned to it. Able to carry tremendous loads, armed with four 20 mm cannon and able to take hits, it was ideal for close support and the vital search-and-rescue mission (SAR). But one of the most important qualities of the Skyraider was its speed — or lack of it. The slow-moving Skyraider was able to track targets more effectively and deliver its ordnance with great accuracy, usually in a single pass. Of course, this came at a cost: from both services, approximately 274 Skyraiders were lost and 114 aviators were killed.

For many, the Skyraider was affectionately known as the "Spad." It was a throwback to a different time, well before supersonic jets ruled the skies. While it may have been old technology, the Skyraider served longer than many of the jet aircraft built to replace it. It was also one of the most versatile aircraft ever built, serving as a ground-attack fighter, airborne early warning, anti-submarine, troop carrier and electronic countermeasures aircraft. Total Skyraider production was 3,180 and ended in 1957.

Right: Flight deck duty aboard an aircraft carrier is extremely hazardous. With catapult steam billowing across the deck and propeller blades whirling, one Navy Skyraider is launched while the other is slowly guided into place.

PILOT'S PERSPECTIVE
Lieutenant Colonel Byron Hukee
USAF (Ret.)

I flew a total of 138 combat missions in the Skyraider in Vietnam. We actually flew four different models. The side-by-side two-seaters were the A-1E and G models, and the single aircraft were the H and the J.

The controls and instrumentation in the Skyraider were pretty much standard. Before it I flew the F-100. But remarkably, the instrumentation in the F-100 and the A-1 were not that dissimilar. The engine instruments and controls were certainly different, but the rest were very similar.

Compared to jet fighters where you had one single-throttle control lever, in the Skyraider you had three: the throttle lever, the prop lever and the mixture lever. Those three had to be used in concert. It was not like a jet where you fire the turbo to start up the engine.

The workload in the Skyraider cockpit was heavy. It was not unusual, when you were learning to fly, to bomb off full pods of rockets instead of shooting them out the front. If you had one switch out of position, the rockets fell away from the wings. As with most aircraft of that era, the only weapons controls on the control column were the bomb and rocket switch. The one up by the trim button in the A-1 was what we called the rocket switch; at the bottom was the bomb switch.

Visibility was different depending if you were flying the E or the H model. Looking out the right side of the E model two-seater was very difficult because you were looking across the cockpit. You were not on the centerline of the aircraft. That forced us, tactically, to fly a lot of left-hand patterns and turns. But in a combat situation, that's obviously not good because you're more predictable. I preferred to fly the single-seat H and J model where the visibility was quite good. The Yankee extraction seat we used was a bit constraining and didn't give us the full 360-degree view.

DOUGLAS A-1H SKYRAIDER
National Museum of Naval Aviation, Pensacola, Florida

1. Elevon Trim
2. Canopy Jettison Switch
3. Canopy Jettison Test Light
4. Wing Flap Control
5. Throttle Control
6. Mixture Control
7. Propeller Control
8. Oxygen Regulator Panel
9. Engine Controls Friction Lock
10. Master Exterior Light Switch
11. Landing Gear Safety Lock
12. Landing Gear Control Release Plunger
13. Landing Gear Control
14. Wheels and Flaps Position Indicator
15. Ignition Switch
16. Water Injection Switch
17. Control Column
18. ECM Control
19. Marker Beacon Audio Switch
20. Marker Beacon Light
21. G-2 Compass Switch
22. Manifold Pressure Gauge
23. Tachometer
24. Torque Pressure Gauge
25. Airspeed Indicator
26. Altimeter
27. AN/APN-22 Radar Altimeter
28. Vertical Gyro Indicator
29. ID-250/ARN Course Indicator
30. Gunsight
31. Magnetic Sump Plugs Warning Light
32. Rate-of-Climb Indicator
33. Turn-and-Bank Indicator
34. Chartboard
35. Armament Panel
36. Rudder Pedal Adjustment Crank
37. Artificial Horizon
38. ID-249/ARN Course Indicator
39. Fuel Quantity Test Switch
40. Windscreen Degreaser
41. ID-310/ARN Range Indicator
42. Fuel Quantity Indicator
43. Engine Gauge Unit
44. Bombs and Rockets Firing Button

Left: An A-1E two-seater Skyraider on the ramp at Bien Hoa, South Vietnam.

LOCKHEED

F-80 SHOOTING STAR

ELEGANT AND CLEAN, THE F-80 SHOOTING STAR WAS THE FIRST USAF AIRCRAFT TO
EXCEED 500 MPH AND THE FIRST TO SHOOT DOWN A SOVIET MiG-15 DURING THE KOREAN WAR.

On November 8, 1950, UN Forces were pushing hard towards the Yalu River, which signified North Korea's border with China. High above the troops, 1st Lieutenant Russell J. Brown was flying an F-80C from Kimpo. Spotting a half-dozen MiG-15s, he and his wingman turned aggressively into the enemy formation. It was the perfect move. The MiG formation was split, sending five scurrying back across the Yalu. A sixth MiG chose to break in the other direction, sealing his fate. Spotting the lone MiG below him, Lieutenant Brown pushed over and dove behind the MiG. With all but one gun jammed, Brown fired a burst of .50-caliber shells that struck the fighter,

sending it spinning to the ground engulfed in flames. This was the world's first jet-versus-jet aerial victory.

The F-80 was in many ways a World War II fighter, but the war ended before it had a chance to see combat. Four YP-80As were sent to Britain and to Italy at the end of 1944 for service trials, but they were never flown in combat. Born out of the design office of Hall Hibbard and Clarence L. "Kelly" Johnson, the F-80 was conceived and built in just 143 days! The first flight of the XP-80 prototype took place on January 8, 1944. While the new engine failed to develop enough power, the new fighter proved faster than any other American fighter, with a maximum speed of 502 mph (808 km/h). America's new fighter proved

The F-80 was an outstanding design in all respects and was the first jet fighter ordered in large numbers by the USAF.

extremely maneuverable and was armed with six .50-caliber machine guns in the nose. By 1945, 563 F-80s had been ordered, but there were problems with the new fighter. By August 1945, eight aircraft had been destroyed and six pilots killed. One of the casualties was the top American ace of World War II, Major Richard Bong. By late 1947, the F-80C was in production. This vastly improved variant equipped fighter units in the United States, Germany and Japan. At the beginning of the Korean War three F-80 Fighter Groups (the 8th, 51st and 49th) were ready for action based in Japan. The war began on June 25, and by June 27 F-80s were flying escort and interceptor missions. It was not an auspicious start. Initially, the F-80C's combat radius was limited, and there were no airfields in Korea capable of handling jets.

Even thought the F-80 had scored the first victory against the swept-wing MiG-15, it was no match for the new Soviet fighter. Relegated to the ground-support role, the F-80 proved a great success and was the best machine in the inventory for strafing. Early in the conflict, the F-80Cs lacked underwing shackles to carry bombs, but they were soon modified to carry two wingtip fuel tanks,

two 1,000-pound bombs and eight underwing rockets. But, as with all early jet fighters, there was a price to be paid. An F-80 fully loaded for a ground-support mission could not carry its full load of 1,800 .50-caliber rounds for its guns. F-80s flew 98,515 combat missions, shooting down 31 enemy aircraft (six of them MiG-15s) and destroying 21 on the ground. They dropped 41,593 tons of bombs and napalm and fired over 81,000 rockets. But the price was heavy. There were 14 F-80s lost in aerial combat, 150 in accidents, and 113 shot down by anti-aircraft fire.

Eventually the F-80 was replaced by the ground-attack version of the F-86, but the F-80 design lived on for decades as the extremely successful T-33 "T-Bird" trainer. The T-33 remained in production until 1959; a total of 6,557 were built. The Royal Canadian Air Force retired their last T-33s in March 2002.

PILOT'S PERSPECTIVE
Brigadier General Robin Olds
USAF (Ret.)

I started flying the P-80 (later designated F-80) in January 1946 and flew it until I went to England to fly the Meteor. Every cockpit had its own individual characteristics, peculiarities and idiotic arrangements. The Brits seemed to have had a blindfolded designer who stood back about ten feet and threw instruments into the cockpit!

For me and my size, the F-80 cockpit was terribly uncomfortable, particularly with the seat chute. It took me a time to take the front part of my parachute and sort of let it sit on the lip of the seat, so there was a backward slant to it.

In the early P-80s, you also had to watch your tail-pipe temperature with an eagle eye as you climbed, because you had to keep reducing throttle to hold it in limits. And for some reason the fuel counter was stuck way down on the very right corner of the instrument panel, and it was one of the most important instruments! Everything else in the cockpit was fine and it was a wonderful instrument airplane. Visibility was excellent. If there was anything I could have changed, it would have been the radio. Right up to the F-4, aircraft designers felt that everything that that had to do with the engine should be grouped around the throttle. The radio stuff was over on the right side, which meant that you had to switch hands in order to work the radio.

Of course, the early P-80s had pressurized cockpits. But it didn't always work. Sometimes a seal would blow and that meant the interior cockpit canopy would completely frost over. It happened more often than not, but fortunately we were all young, dumb and healthy.

Those of us who flew the early jets went through a lot of trauma. The early ejection seats were horrible and often didn't work. We preferred to fly with the safety pins in and pull them out quickly if we had to bail out. In the early P-80s we didn't have ejection seats. If you had to get out and you had any kind of control, you unstrapped, got rid of the canopy, pulled back on the stick a bit and then jammed it forward. That would shoot the airplane away and down from you. It was something the Germans used to do back in World War II.

LOCKHEED F-80C SHOOTING STAR
USAF Museum, Dayton, Ohio

1. Oxygen Regulator
2. Ejection Seat Handle
3. Circuit Breakers
4. Fuel Tank Selector Switch
5. Fuel Tanks Indicator Lights
6. Elevator Tabs Override Switch
7. Fuel Filter De-Icing Switch
8. Radio Control Panel
9. Emergency Fuel Switch
10. Fluid Injection Switch
11. Wing Flaps Switch
12. Wing Flaps Position Indicator
13. Starting Fuel Switch
14. Air Start Ignition Switch
15. Throttle with Microphone Button
16. Throttle Friction Control Knob
17. JATO Jettison Handle
18. Landing Gear Horn Cut-out Button
19. Light
20. Cockpit Ram Air Ventilator
21. Aileron Boost Shut-off
22. Hydrofuse Reset Handle
23. Accelerometer
24. Oxygen Flow Indicator
25. Gunsight
26. Landing Gear Position Indicators
27. Fluid Injection Pressure Gauge
28. Turn-and-Slip Indicator
29. Altimeter
30. Oxygen Pressure Gauge
31. Attitude Indicator
32. Airspeed Indicator
33. Emergency Fuel System Indicator Lights
34. Gunsight Light Rheostat
35. Check List
36. Vertical Velocity Indicator
37. Elevon Trim Control
38. Clock
39. Hydraulic System Pressure Gauge
40. Elevator Tab Neutral Indicator Light
41. Radio Compass
42. Control Column
43. Directional Indicator
44. Exhaust Gas Temp
45. Parking Brake Handle
46. Fuel Quantity Gauge
47. Fuel Quantity Counter
48. Gyro Instrument Warning Light
49. Direction Indicator Reset Button
50. Radio Compass Indicator
51. Engine Fuel Pressure Gauge
52. Fuel Quantity Warning Light
53. JATO Arming Switch and Warning Light

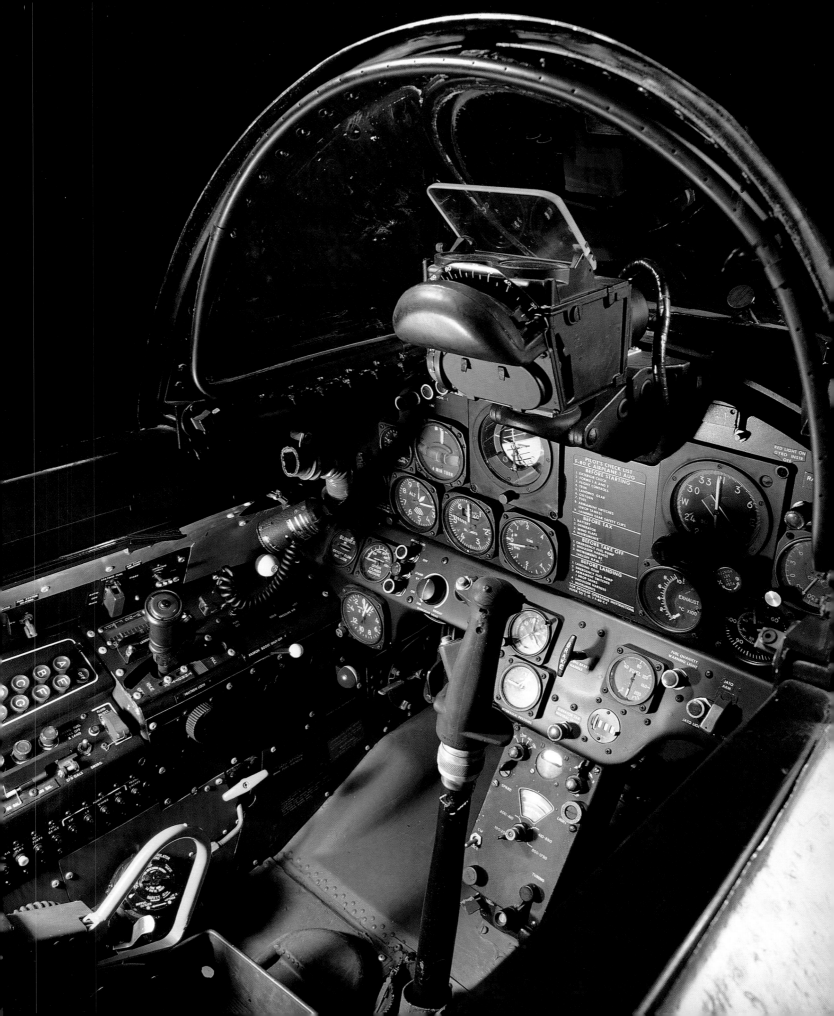

F-84 THUNDERJET

As P-47s FLEW THEIR LAST COMBAT MISSIONS OF WORLD WAR II, THE DESIGNERS
AT REPUBLIC WERE BUSY PUTTING THE FINISHING TOUCHES ON ONE OF
AMERICA'S MOST SUCCESSFUL FIGHTERS OF THE COLD WAR.

At the end of the Second World War, American jet-fighter aircraft design and production was just beginning. One company at the forefront was Republic, with its new F-84 design. In the early stages, the Republic designers considered simply installing a jet engine into an existing P-47 Thunderbolt airframe. This idea was quickly scrapped and the F-84 began again with a clean sheet of paper. The F-84 was a cantilever low-wing monoplane, with straight, laminar-flow wings and cantilevered horizontal tailplanes mounted halfway up the vertical fin. The F-84 was all metal with a duralumin skin and was the first American jet fighter with the air inlet for the turbine engine located in the nose. The new fighter, with its clean, straightforward lines, was well received at USAAF's Material Division, which ordered three prototypes and 400 series aircraft. On February 28, 1946, Major William A. Lien took off from Muroc Dry Lake in the first XP-84, the first American fighter to make its maiden flight after the Second World War. It was powered by a 3,750-pound (1,700 kg) General Electric J35 turbojet. On September 7, 1946, the XP-84 also set a new American speed record of 611 mph (983 km/h), only to have it snatched away that very same day by a Gloster Meteor over England.

With the coming of victory in Europe and the Pacific, the USAAF suspended its earlier order of 400 P-84s, replacing it with an order for 15 YP-84A

The F-84 was the chief Allied fighter-bomber in Korea. This example belongs to the 14th Fighter Group.

preseries aircraft and 85 series P-84Bs on January 15, 1946. The 15 YP-84As were delivered for evaluation by the USAAF, and by April 1947, the aircraft were approved. Production of the P-84B, redesignated F-84B in mid-1948, totaled 226 aircraft. These were followed by 191 F-84Cs and 154 F-84Ds — all powered by the more powerful Allison J35 turbojet engine. Next up was the F-84E. This version with a stretched fuselage had a longer range, radar and increased stores and armament provisions. There were 843 of them built; 100 of these new fighters were the first Thunderjets to enter service with America's NATO allies. The F-84E was followed by the G model, of which 1,936 were built. The G had the honor of being the last straight-wing fighter-bomber to be deployed by both Strategic Air Command and Tactical Air Command.

In December 1950, five months after the beginning of the Korean War, the F-84 had its first taste of combat. F-84Es of the 27th Fighter Escort Wing flew their first mission and were soon joined by the 49th, 58th, and the 474th Fighter Groups. Used at first as a bomber escort fighter, the F-84 was quickly outclassed when the swept-wing MiG-15 appeared. The F-84 units were quickly switched to the fighter-bomber role, and armed with two 1,000-pound (455 kg) bombs and six .50-caliber machine guns. There they served with outstanding effect, earning widespread respect for effectiveness over the battlefield. In May 1953, in two spectacular operations, 59 F-84Gs attacked the Toksan Dike on May 13, and on May 16, 90 Thunderjets successfully carried out the attack on Chusan. At the end of the Korean War, the F-84 ranked as one of the world's best ground-attack fighters. Progress on a swept-wing version was well in hand, and on June 3, 1950, the F-84F Thunderstreak took to the air. Production began in 1952 and did not end until 1958, when 2,711 Thunderstreaks had been built. At the same time 718 photo-reconnaissance aircraft were built under the designation RF-84F and named Thunderflash.

In the end, all three versions of the F-84 not only served with the USAF, but saw extensive service with the air forces of Belgium, Denmark, France, West Germany, Greece, Italy, Norway, the Netherlands, Portugal and Turkey.

PILOT'S PERSPECTIVE
Joe Jackson
USAF (Ret.)

The cockpit of the F-84 had a pretty standard layout as far as the instruments and controls were concerned. I thought it quite practical. There was adequate space and it was very comfortable. Of course, all the fighters were too small for long-distance flights. Progressing from a piston-engine fighter to a jet, one of the first things you noticed was the smoothness of the engine. There was a distinct lack of vibration, noise and the rattling of pistons flopping up and down. The visibility from the F-84 was excellent, but not nearly as good as in the late-model jets such as the F-16 and F-15. But it was very good. The first F-84s had a bubble canopy, but then they suffered from canopy blow-outs. I think the first one occurred in 1950. This poor guy was just flying along when the canopy blew out. It ripped his helmet off and knocked him unconscious. When he finally came to, he was lolly-gagging around the sky, zooming and diving, and was lost as all-get-out. He had no way to navigate. His maps were gone and he had no radio. He managed to land on a road in Texas. They then replaced the canopy, put some fuel in the plane and he took off. There were a couple of other blow-outs after that, so they put the ribbed canopy on the aircraft.

There's nothing really that I would have changed in the cockpit, but I would have given the F-84 more power and a better wing so it would go faster. The F-84 seemed to roll on the ground for a long time before getting airborne.

I flew 107 combat missions in the F-84 during the Korean War. We all got shot up quite often. The F-84 came equipped with armor plate behind the cockpit, but that's all there was to protect us. If you were using it for interdiction and close support, the F-84 was very good. If you were going to use it for air-to-air combat, I would say it was poor. Especially against the MiG-15. The MiG-15 was lighter, more maneuverable, and it could out-turn the F-84. We only had one advantage, and that was with our aileron boost ratio cranked up to 10 to 1. We could outroll them. We could reverse our turns a lot quicker. If they got into a firing position, we could do a snap turn and get away from them and maybe even roll back in time to get a shot. But that didn't happen very often.

REPUBLIC F-84E THUNDERJET
USAF Museum, Dayton, Ohio

1. Tip Tank Empty Indicator Lights and Switches
2. Fuel Selector Control
3. Throttle
4. Cockpit Light
5. Landing Gear Warning Horn Release Switch
6. Landing Gear Emergency Uplock Release
7. Landing Light Switch
8. Landing Gear Control
9. Emergency Fuel Switches
10. Landing Gear Ground Retract Switch
11. Slaved Gyro Slaving Switch
12. Slaved Gyro Compass Switch
13. Rocket/Dive Angle Control
14. Accelerometer
15. Radio Compass
16. Accelerometer
17. Bomb Target Wind Control
18. Airspeed Indicator
19. Engine Fuel Light
20. Hydraulic Pressure Gauge
21. Span Adjustment Dial
22. Canopy Control Switch
23. Engine Overheat Warning Light
24. Wing Tank Pump Pressure Light
25. Manual Tip Tank Release
26. Control Stick
27. Gunsight
28. Engine Fire Warning Light
29. Gyro Compass
30. Turn-and-Bank Indicator
31. Fuel Level Indicator
32. Target Indicator Light
33. Radar Range Sweep Control
34. Attitude Indicator
35. Rate-of-Climb Indicator
36. Low Fuel Level Warning Light
37. Engine Oil Pressure Gauge
38. Sight Filament Switches
39. Tachometer
40. Exhaust Temp Gauge
41. Fuel Pressure Warning Light
42. Fuel Pressure Gauge
43. Dimmer Control
44. Fuel Flow Instrument
45. Inverter Failure Light
46. Instrument Power Switch
47. Generator Over-Voltage Light
48. Generator Switches
49. Ammeter
50. Cockpit Altimeter
51. Oxygen Regulator
52. Oxygen Control Panel
53. Ejection Seat Handle
54. Rudder Pedals

NORTH AMERICAN
F-86 SABRE

U.S. FIGHTER PILOTS ENTERED THE KOREAN WAR WITH FAR MORE EXPERIENCE
THAN THEY HAD EARLY IN WORLD WAR II, AND THE ONE AIRCRAFT THAT WOULD MATCH
AND THEN EXCEED THE PERFORMANCE OF THE DEADLY MiG-15 — THE F-86 SABRE.

Without a doubt, of all the fighters built during the 1950s, the F-86 Sabre ranks as number one. While its archrival, the MiG-15, was built in greater numbers, it always came off second-best in combat with the Sabre.

During the latter half of the Second World War, North American Aviation quickly established itself as a first-rate producer of fighters with the war-winning P-51 Mustang. Designers at North American watched the emergence of jet propulsion with great interest and sketched several single- and twin-fuselage "jet Mustangs" in 1943–44. These were quickly dropped, and in collaboration with the Army Air Force (AAF) and U.S. Navy, an all-jet fighter was proposed. The result for the Navy was the NA-134, which became the FJ-1 Fury, and the NA-140 for the Air Force. Although it was started later than the Navy NA-134, the NA-140 was actually under contract first. On August 30, 1944, the AAF ordered two prototypes with the designation XP-86. Both of these aircraft had straight laminar-flow wings. While construction of the prototypes was underway, the design team at North American received the first reports on German swept-wing design. Inspired by this new data, North American incorporated the new swept wing in the XP-86. The U.S. Navy was not as adventurous, but the U.S. Air Force agreed to the swept-wing proposal, and on October 1, 1947, the XP-86 flew for the first time. The test-flight results were extremely positive, and in April 1948, the XP-86 broke the sound barrier in a dive and became the first American fighter to achieve this.

In June 1948 the "pursuit" designation was changed to "fighter," so the new swept-wing fighter became the F-86A Sabre. By the end of 1949, two fighter groups (1st and 4th) were fully equipped the beautiful new F-86. Powered by a 5,200-pound (2,840 kg) GE J47 jet engine, armed with six 0.5-inch-caliber (12.7 mm) machine guns and equipped with a radar-ranging gunsight, the F-86 was the most potent fighter in the world. But on June 25, 1950, that would all change. The invasion of South Korea by North Korea caught the Americans by complete surprise. Even more surprising was the appearance of the swept-wing MiG-15 in November. Both the F-80 Shooting Star and F-84 Thunderjet were no match for the superlative Soviet fighter. At first little attention was paid to the new and lethal fighter, but when fifty divisions of Chinese troops attacked across the front, the call went out for the F-86. The 4th Fighter Interceptor Wing was the first was the first to fly combat missions with the F-86. It quickly became apparent that the F-86A could not fly as high as the MiG-15 (the F-86 could barely reach 42,000 feet while the MiG-15 could cruise at 50,000 feet). In some ways the MiG-15 was markedly superior to the F-86, but the biggest difference between the two fighters was in pilot quality and attitude. Here the Americans were superior. Although outnumbered during the entire Korean War, F-86 pilots claimed 792 MiG-15s for a loss of just 78 Sabres.

After the war, the USAF claims fell to 379 MiGs with a loss of 103 F-86s. While this figure is considerably lower than first claimed, it is generally accepted that the F-86 achieved a victory-loss ratio of at least four to one. Regardless of the exact numbers, that is a remarkable feat of arms. Production of the F-86 reached 8,681, and no fewer than 26 countries have used the legendary Sabre, including the RAF and RCAF.

Left: The Canadair-built Sabre proved a great success. Powered by the Orenda 14 engine, the Canadair Sabre 6 was considered the best Sabre ever built. Here three factory-fresh Sabres pose for the camera.

PILOT'S PERSPECTIVE
Colonel Walker M. Mahurin
USAF (Ret.)

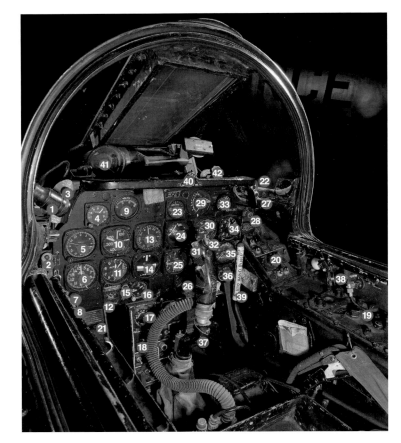

I don't know when it was exactly when I first flew the F-86, but I think it was in 1948. Before that I flew Mustangs and Thunderbolts in World War II, and the P-80 jet after the war.

The cockpit in the F-86 was fine, but the exciting thing was it had a swept wing and it could go like hell. The F-86 had a very comfortable cockpit because you could turn the temperature down and get snow coming out of the air conditioning! You could also get heat that was comfortable. Remember, in the F-86 you weren't going to be flying sixteen to eighteen hours the way they do now. Over Korea we'd fly two-and-a-half-hour missions.

The difference between the F-86 and MiG-15 was that the F-86 was a Cadillac and the MiG was an early Ford. The MiG didn't have boosted controls and they didn't have air conditioning in the cockpit. The cockpit of the MiG was small, and for large Americans, your feet were sort of tucked up underneath you. It also had some serious control problems.

The controls and instruments in the F-86 were close to hand and easy reach. The instruments were all suitably placed. The landing-gear lever had a wheel on it so you couldn't grab something else and think you were lowering or raising the landing gear. The dive brakes were handy on the throttle. The visibility was good, but you couldn't see out the back end because there was armor plate right behind you and radio stuff in the back end of the canopy. The gunsight on the F-86 was much better than on the MiG-15s. It was radar ranging and would track a target from a pretty far distance out. The MiG-15 pilots were using more or less World War II gunsights.

I think the F-86 was one of the finest airplanes our country ever had. Every airplane had a few undesirable characteristics, but the 86 was able to expand to become the F-86D. The best F-86s were the ones built by the Canadians, equipped with the Orenda engine. They could go faster, longer and higher, and were better than the ones we had down here.

NORTH AMERICAN F-86A SABRE
USAF Museum, Dayton, Ohio

1. Fluorescent Light
2. Landing Gear Emergency Up Button
3. Emergency Fuel Switch
4. Accelerometer
5. Radio Compass Indicator
6. Machmeter
7. Generator Overvoltage Warning Light
8. Inverter Warning Light
9. Volt Meter
10. Airspeed Indicator
11. Altimeter
12. Generator Voltage Indicator
13. Directional Indicator
14. Turn-and-Slip Indicator
15. Generator Warning Light
16. Clock
17. Weapons Selector
18. Armament Panel
19. Radio Compass Control Panel
20. Forward Console
21. Rudder Pedal
22. Fire Warning Lights
23. Horizontal Stabilizer Position Indicator
24. Attitude Indicator
25. Vertical Velocity Indicator
26. Utility Hydraulic Pressure Gauge
27. Canopy Alternate Emergency Jettison Handle
28. Fire Warning System Test Button
29. Exhaust Temperature Gauge
30. Tachometer
31. Gun Button
32. Trim Control
33. Cockpit Air Temperature Gauge
34. Cabin Pressure Altimeter
35. Fuel Quantity Gauge
36. Oil Pressure Gauge
37. Control Column
38. Fluorescent Light
39. Emergency Hydraulic Hand-Pump
40. Radar Target Indicator
41. Sight Range Dial
42. Reticle Dimmer Knob

This Canadair-built Sabre is just one of the 1,815 built by the Montreal-based company.

NORTH AMERICAN

F-100 SUPER SABRE

GAPE-MOUTHED WITH A SLIGHTLY ARCHED APPEARANCE, THE F-100 REPRESENTED
A WHOLE NEW ERA OF UNBRIDLED SPEED. THE LOW-DRAG, ULTRA STREAMLINED FUSELAGE
AND THIN, HIGHLY SWEPT WING PRODUCED THE WORLD'S FIRST SUPERSONIC FIGHTER.

North American Aviation, the same stable that produced the war-winning P-51 Mustang and the F-86 Sabre, would accomplish a new first with the remarkable F-100 — the first of the "Century Series" of fighters. In 1949, North American began design studies for an improved F-86 with a 45-degree angle sweep on the wings, powered by the new Pratt & Whitney jet engine with three times the power of the F-86. The goal was to produce a fighter capable of supersonic speeds in level flight. The USAF ordered two prototypes as well as 110 series aircraft of the newly designated YF-100 on November 1, 1951.

Powered by a two-stage Pratt & Whitney J57-P-7 engine with afterburner, the new cantilever low-wing monoplane with a 45-degree sweep took to the air for

the first time on May 25, 1953. Christened the Super Sabre, the YF-100A broke the sound barrier on its first flight and ushered in a new era of fighter combat. The flight tests went well, and the Super Sabre went into full production shortly after.

Many "firsts" were attributed to the F-100. On October 14, 1953, the world speed record was broken in the first YF-100A, with speeds reaching 755.149 mph (1,215 km/h). Two years later an F-100C did even better, achieving a speed of 822.135 mph (1,323 km/h). For all the glory, however, there were some serious problems with the world's first supersonic fighter. Landing the F-100 was described as "a sort of controlled crash." After a series of accidents and the death of test pilot George Welch, the 479th Fighter Group was

Below: A formation of F-100s head for a suspected Viet Cong position somewhere in South Vietnam. Above right: From the pilot's perspective — a formation of F-100s prepares to land at Tan Son Nhut Air Base in South Vietnam, March 1966.

ordered to ground its F-100s. It was the most serious setback for a Western fighter program since the end of the Second World War. After a month of intensive investigation, it was discovered that the tailplane fin was not large or strong enough. Under certain flight conditions, the tailplane failed, causing the aircraft to crash. Aircraft that were currently in production had their fin and rudders increased in size by 27 percent, and all aircraft already delivered were similarly modified.

By February 1955, the F-100 was cleared and put back into service. By this time, 203 F-100As had left the assembly line and production had begun on the F-100C fighter-bomber version. This variant had six wing pylons for bombs and missiles along with the four Pontiac M-39, 20 mm revolver cannons. The next version, designated the F-100D, was also a fighter-bomber. This version was equipped with the LABS (Low Altitude Bombing System) and in-flight refueling. The majority of F-100 units were based in the United States, but five fighter groups were assigned to NATO in Europe.

The first time F-100s fired their guns in combat was during the Vietnam War. By this time the Super Sabre was gradually being replaced by the F-105 Thunderchief and the F-4 Phantom, but regardless, four Super Sabre Wings would prove their worth from 1966 until 1971. Indeed, the Third Tactical Fighter Bomber Wing completed more than 100,000 missions before the end of 1969.

The F-100 remained in service until 1980, when the last five Air National Guard groups gave up their mounts and converted to the A-10 and Corsair II. The F-100 also flew with the French, Danish and Turkish air forces. In all, 2,294 Super Sabres were built.

PILOT'S PERSPECTIVE

George Day
USAF (Ret.)

I first flew the F-100 in the early spring of 1956. I thought the F-100 had a very splendid cockpit display. Everything was in front of both of your elbows They thought out the cockpit really well and, although you had a lot of really complicated exotic stuff in it, it nevertheless was a very pleasing layout. It had a great gyro called the MM1 attitude gyro. I was very interested in that because we were doing a lot of 4G Immelmanns in the soup off of the deck and I could see that it was going to be a beauty.

I found the comfort level in the F-100 excellent. The seat was wide. The armrests were in a good position. We had a backpack in the airplane that strapped to the dinghy and the seat, and it was a very comfortable backpack and seat. The visibility from the F-100 was just smashing. It wasn't as good as the F-16, but it was probably the best visibility airplane on the market at that time. The environmental controls in the F-100 were excellent. Although the first time you saw one, it looked a little goofy, it was a great bird. It was well engineered. Ergonomically and cosmetically, it was about as close to perfect as any airplane we had at that time.

A bombed-up F-100D at an airbase in South Vietnam. A total of 186 F-100s were shot down during the Vietnam War, all by anti-aircraft fire and small-arms fire.

I flew about 140 combat missions in Vietnam. The workload for the pilot in combat was minimal. Every one of our flights in combat was long distance. We would refuel about twice in the air and, depending on how much burner we used, our flights would last up to five and half hours.

I had 2,200 hours in the F-100. The F-100 had an automatic pilot, but we disconnected them for safety reasons. On long-distance flights you had to fly the airplane all the way. It was really quite fatiguing because, one thing about the F-100 — it never had quite enough rudder. They put in a yaw damper, but they never got it quite right.

The F-105 was famous for being the toughest airplane flown in Vietnam, but I know the F-100 was just a rugged as the 105.

NORTH AMERICAN F-100C SUPER SABRE
USAF Museum, Dayton, Ohio

1. Sight Selector Unit
2. Standby Attitude Indicator
3. Clock
4. Arresting Hook Release Button
5. Drop Tank Fuel Quantity Test Switch
6. Fuel Quantity Gauge
7. Fuel Quantity Gauge
8. Drag Chute Handle
9. Command Radio Channel Indicator
10. AC Loadmeter
11. Airspeed/Machmeter

12. Altimeter
13. Radio Magnetic Indicator
14. Special Store Unlock Handle
15. In-Flight Control Test Panel
16. RAWH Indicators
17. Gun and Missile Camera Controls
18. Heading Indicator
19. Course Indicator
20. TACAN Range Indicator
21. Master Caution Light
22. Attitude Indicator
23. Vertical Velocity Indicator

24. Fuel Quantity Gauge Forward Tank
25. Control Column
26. Attitude Indicator Fast Erection Button
27. Fire and Overheat Warning Lights
28. Turn-and-Slip Indicator
29. Bombs and Rockets Firing Button
30. Elevator Trim Control
31. Gunsight Gaging Button
32. Hydraulic Pressure Gauge Switch
33. Accelerometer

34. LABS Release Indicator Light
35. Cockpit Pressure Altitude Indicator
36. Fuel Flow Indicator
37. Hydraulic Pressure Gauge
38. Oil Pressure Gauge
39. Exhaust Temp Gauge
40. Tachometer
41. Engine Pressure Ratio Gauge
42. Indicator and Caution Light Panel
43. Electrical Control Panel
44. Landing Gear Emergency Lowering Handle

45. Liquid Oxygen Quantity Gauge
46. Oxygen Regulator Control Panel
47. Canopy Emergency Jettison Handle
48. Lighting Control Panel
49. Radio Compass Control Panel
50. TACAN Control Panel
51. J-4 Compass Control Panel
52. Air Conditioning Control Panel
53. Standby Compass

McDONNELL

F-101 VOODOO

ORIGINALLY DESIGNED AS A LONG-RANGE ESCORT FIGHTER, THE F-101 VOODOO WAS VERSATILE ENOUGH TO SERVE WITH ALL THREE U.S. AIR FORCE COMMANDS — STRATEGIC, TACTICAL AND AIR DEFENSE.

The Korean War brought into sharp focus the need for the U.S. Air Force to have a new long-range escort fighter or "penetration fighter." The idea for such a long-range jet escort fighter was first issued as far back as 1945, when McDonnell produced the XF-88. The XF-88 first flew on October 20, 1948, and was given a clean bill of health, but its speed was disappointing. By June 1950 the new fighter was close to being scrapped, but events in Korean highlighted the need for a modern, long-range escort fighter. The XF-88 seemed to offer the most potential, and McDonnell received an order for two prototypes, designated F-101 Voodoo. The new F-101 differed from the XF-88 in many respects: the fuselage was stretched and made wider to accommodate the new J57-P-13 engines and to allow more room for fuel. The wing and

air intakes had been enlarged, and the tail assembly was higher, with the tailplane positioned near the top of the fin. The new aircraft was to be equipped with APS-54 radar and armed with four 20 mm cannons, three Falcon missiles and twelve rockets.

On September 29, 1954, the F-101 project suffered a major setback when Strategic Air Command lost interest in the project. While the F-101 had good range, it could not escort SAC's bombers safely to their targets. But there was a role for the Voodoo with the Tactical Air Command, which requested a fighter-bomber version of the new fighter. The first 77 F-101As turned out to be hybrid aircraft fitted with APS-54 radar as well as LADD (Low Altitude Drogued Delivery). The next batch were the real thing, with strengthened wings and wing pylons for bombs, both nuclear and

Above: A CF-101 Voodoo launches a Genie nuclear air-to-air missile minus the warhead.
Above right: Canada's cold winter climate required special clothing. These toque-wearing aircrew scramble to their CF-101s.

conventional. The F-101 was also being developed as an unarmed photo-reconnaissance aircraft. The first flight of the reconnaissance version flew on June 30, 1955. The RF-101 was the USAF's first supersonic photo-reconnaissance fighter and proved of immense value during the Cuban Missile Crisis.

For a fighter that was initially rejected, the F-101 managed quite well. It slowly worked its way back into the USAF inventory. In 1953 the Air Defense Command decided that it needed a certain number of all-weather interceptors in case there were delays with

the Convair F-102 and F-106 programs. The F-101 was modified to become a two-seat all-weather interceptor with no guns, but stores consisting of two MB-1 Genie nuclear missiles mounted externally and three Falcon missiles carried internally. A total of 480 "replacement" Voodoos made it off the assembly lines.

One of the most outstanding features of the F-101 was its safety record. During the F-101's long career it had the lowest accident-to-number-of-hours-flown ratio, and that record includes it extensive use as a photo-reconnaissance aircraft in the hostile environment of the Vietnam War. In 1961, the Royal Canadian Air Force took delivery of 66 CF-101B/CF-101Fs to enhance the air defense of North America. Five squadrons — the 409, 410, 414, 416 and 425 — were equipped with the type until 1983. Twenty-five F-101s were also supplied to Taiwan.

The F-101 Voodoo remained in front-line service with the USAF for fourteen years before serving another eight with the Air National Guard until 1975. Built in relatively small numbers — there were only 805 produced — the F-101 Voodoo proved to be one of the most valuable fighters of the Cold War.

PILOT'S PERSPECTIVE
Major Stan Jaknunas
RCAF (Ret.)

The first trip I took in a Voodoo was in the autumn of 1972. It was with Operational Training Squadron 410 out of Bagotville. I transitioned from the T-33, F-86 and Tutor.

The Voodoo cockpit was extremely large compared to those of jets I had flown before, especially the Sabre, which was very cramped. There was a lot of elbow room. It was like sitting in an office.

A long flight in the Voodoo was around two hours. That was either in an exercise where you were flying in a CAP (combat air patrol), waiting for a target to come down from the north or if you flew into a place like Goose Bay. Most of the exercises we flew were at night, and the cockpit was so comfortable you could almost fall asleep. The only real problem I had was with the cockpit seals. They created havoc with pressurization. On one mission I put my map against the canopy railing and it was sucked right out of the cockpit.

The controls and instruments were easy to reach and very ergonomic. Some of the circuit breakers and switches were a little far back, but the worst ones were the SAG (semi-auto ground environment) systems. Those were hard to see because you had to turn your head and look back. Visibility from the cockpit was good. It would have been nice to have a heads-up display, but that was before its time.

The workload was manageable except when you were doing a front supersonic intercept. The target was coming at you at 15 miles a minute — you were going toward it at 15 miles a minute, and the radar had only a 30-mile capability! You had approximately one minute to acquire your target, track it, get your weapons prepared, fire and get out of the way.

The cockpit lighting was a little on the dark side, and from time to time, you would lose a light on the instrument panel, but that wasn't a problem, because at night we always carried a flashlight.

McDONNELL F-101B VOODOO
USAF Museum, Dayton, Ohio

1. Automatic Pilot Function Selector Panel
2. Throttle Control Levers
3. Internal Air Starter Switch
4. Icing Ignition Switch
5. Hydraulic Pressure Gauge (Utility)
6. Emergency Speed Brake Switch
7. Engine Fuel Control Switch
8. Wing Flap Position Indicator
9. Landing Gear Control Panel
10. Emergency Brake Handle
11. Hydraulic Pressure Gauge (Primary)
12. Landing Gear Warning Light
13. Accelerometer
14. Pitch Boundary Indicator
15. Standby Attitude Indicator
16. Attack Scope
17. Take-off Trim Panel
18. Exhaust Temp Indicators
19. Turn-and-Slip Indicator
20. Arresting Hook Control
21. True Airspeed Indicator
22. Standby Turn-and-Slip Indicator
23. Armament Control Panel
24. Command Mach Indicator
25. Airspeed and Mach Indicator
26. Bearing Distance Heading Indicator
27. Attitude Indicator
28. Engine Tachometers
29. Elevator Trim Control
30. Altimeter
31. Course Indicator
32. Rate-of-Climb Indicator
33. Engine Oil Pressure
34. ILS TACAN Switch
35. Ejection Racks Lock Panel
36. Pilot's Scope Control Panel
37. Control Column
38. Standby Compass Light Switch
39. Rudder Pedal Control
40. Compass
41. Gunsight

Left: An RCAF Voodoo touches down with drag chute fully deployed.

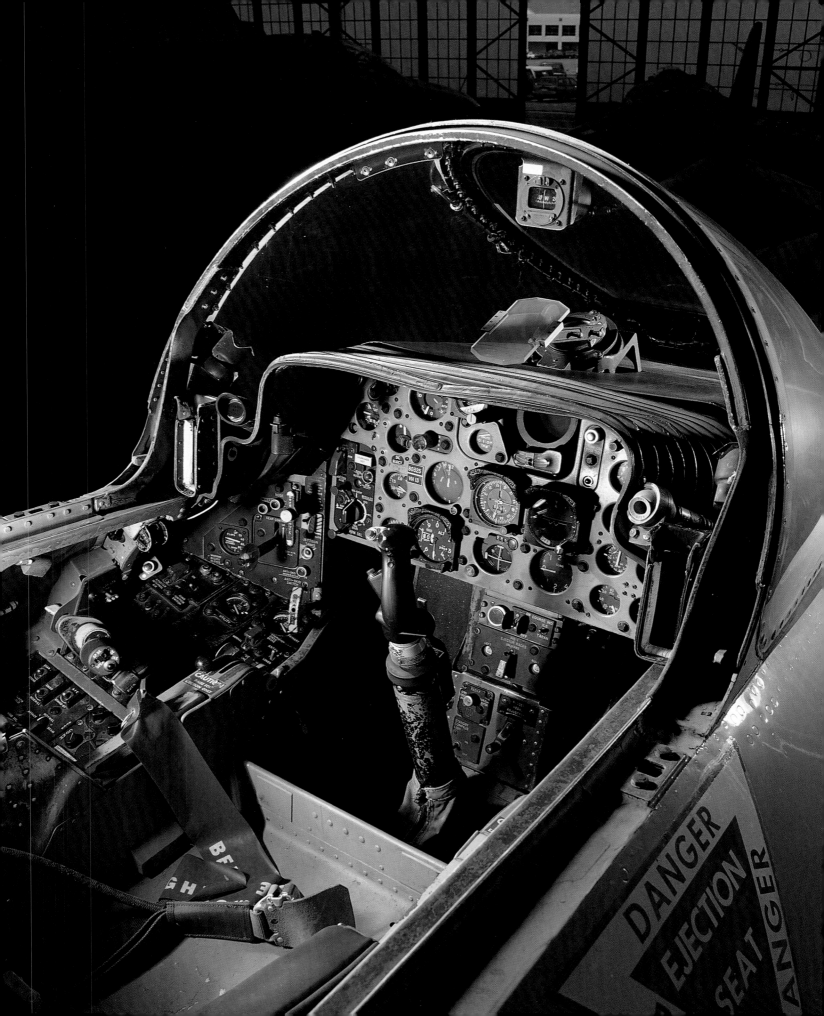

McDONNELL

F-4 PHANTOM

THE F-4 PHANTOM WAS A LEGEND IN ITS OWN TIME. IT WAS THE SECOND-MOST WIDELY PRODUCED WESTERN FIGHTER, ONLY OUTNUMBERED BY THE SABRE, AND WAS THE FIRST AND ONLY FIGHTER DESIGNED FOR THE U.S. NAVY ORDERED BY THE USAF.

Described as a masterpiece of aero-engineering, the F-4 Phantom is truly one of the greatest fighters of the Cold War. When it first appeared in May 1958, the F-4 was the fourth McDonnell fighter to go into series production for the U.S. Navy.

Throughout 1952, the McDonnell Aircraft Corporation was focused on the development of a supersonic shipboard jet fighter in anticipation of winning the U.S. Navy supersonic fighter design competition. It was believed that company's track record of 1,000 naval fighters built (FH-1 Phantom, F2H Banshee, F3H Demon) and the work done on the supersonic F-101 Voodoo would greatly enhance its chances. But when the contract was awarded to Chance Vought and the F8U Crusader, the shock was complete. The F8U was an ambitious design and one that McDonnell realized could end its role as the supplier of shipboard fighters for the U.S. Navy. In mid-1953, McDonnell dug in and took the first steps that eventually lead to an aeronautic pot of gold. In a company-funded project, McDonnell engineers canvassed U.S. Navy operations personnel, the Bureau of Aeronautics and the Chief of Naval Operations. Anyone who had an opinion about the requirements for the next-generation carrier-based aircraft was asked about it and their comments were duly noted. Shortly afterward, a mockup of the F3H-G/H fighter-bomber was unveiled. The Navy was impressed and ordered two prototypes. Incredibly, however, in May 1955, the U.S. Navy changed its mind: it now wanted a long range, high-level, all-weather interceptor instead of a fighter-bomber. Two weeks of frenzied activity changed the F3H into the F4H-1 fighter. It was a major redesign. Four Sparrow missiles were added along with a second crew member to operate the fire-control system.

On May 27, 1958, the first flight of the F-4 Phantom took place. Widely regarded as an ugly duckling, the F-4 still had to prove itself against the Chance Vought F8U-3. In the end, the Navy chose the F-4 Phantom and ordered 649 aircraft. Even before carrier trials were set to begin in February 1960, the Phantom had already set fifteen speed and altitude records. When flown against a USAF Convair F-106, the F-4 proved the better airplane in almost all respects and 582 were ordered by the U.S. Air Force. Thus began an unprecedented building boom for the F-4 Phantom. Production rates rose considerably during the Vietnam War, where the F-4 was used by the USAF, U.S. Navy and Marine Corps. The first Phantoms to see combat belonged to Navy Squadrons VF-142 and VF-143 aboard the carrier USS Constellation. Phantoms interceptors and fighter-bombers saw heavy service throughout the Vietnam War and were credited with 277 combat victories. Two Phantom aces would emerge from the conflict each with five victories — Navy Lieutenants Randy Cunningham and William Driscoll and Air Force Captains Steve Ritchie and Charles DeBellevue. By the end of the Vietnam War, U.S. aircraft had shot down 192 MiGs — 75 percent of them were claimed by Phantom drivers.

The Americans were not the only ones to see the value of the Phantom. Export orders accounted for 22 percent of all Phantoms built, with sales to West Germany (273), Israel (240), Iran (218), Japan (151), South Korea (72), Turkey (48), Spain (36), Egypt (35), Australia (24), and Greece (20). Great Britain was the only other nation to fly the F-4 from a carrier deck and ordered 52 F-4s powered by Rolls-Royce Spey turbofans. In all, over 5,000 F-4 Phantoms were built.

Right: Armed with laser-guided bombs, three F-4s of the 8th Tactical Fighter Wing head out for another bombing mission over South Vietnam.

PILOT'S PERSPECTIVE
Congressman Randy Cunningham
U.S. Navy

Currently I'm flying the F-15 at Edwards Air Force Base and the F-18E/F down at Pax. In flight training I flew the T-34, then went to the T-2, the F9 Cougar and then onto Miramar for the Phantom.

The cockpit in the F-4 was very roomy, but I preferred the tight-fitting cockpit in the A-4 Skyhawk. It was like a part of your soul. But when it came to night flying around a carrier, I preferred the F-4. The roominess of the F-4 allowed me to look around the cockpit without having to move my body. In the A-4, I couldn't do that. I thought the instrument and controls were in good positions for the time of the aircraft. Remember, the F-4 was built as an interceptor. There weren't going to be anymore dogfights. It was designed to use its radar. One of the best things in the Phantom cockpit was the repeater radar scope in the front seat. It gave me a situational awareness I would not have had without it. Quite frankly, we didn't use the radar that much in Vietnam. All five of my kills were close in, using Sidewinders.

I thought the instruments and controls were fairly well engineered and placed compared to in other airplanes. I guess the hardest thing to do in the cockpit was operate the weapons-management system. You had to know what you were doing. It was training and switchology. I had a cockpit setup in my car. When I drove along and I'd see an airliner I drilled myself. The cockpit was relatively easy for me because I worked it so hard. Different cockpits have varying degrees of difficulty or capability. It's up to the pilot to train in the cockpit to make it easier or hard.

Visibility was not as good as the say the F-16, but it was a lot better than a MiG-17, 19 or 21. We also had another pair of eyes with the RIO (Radar Intercept Officer) in back. The good thing was, our squadron believed in flying with the same RIO.

The one thing the Navy F-4s didn't have was a gun. When you had a MiG on your wingman's tail and if he was close in, you knew that your missile wouldn't know the good guy from the bad. But if you had a gun, he'd have to honor that. Twice I ended up zooming and coming up to a MiG that didn't even know I was there, but I couldn't shoot him because I was too close for a missile shot.

McDONNELL F-4J PHANTOM
American Air Museum, Duxford, England

1. Flap Control Panel
2. Fuel Control Panel
3. Rudder Trim Switch
4. Throttles
5. Engine Control Panel (Outboard)
6. Engine Control Panel (Inbound)
7. Boost Pump Check Switches
8. Boost Pump Gauge
9. Boost Pump Gauge
10. Oxygen Pressure Gauge
11. Canopy Emergency Jettison Handle
12. Landing Gear Position Indicators
13. Stabilizer Trim Indicator
14. Cabin Altimeter
15. Landing Gear Control Handle
16. Flap Position Indicators
17. Emergency AIL Droop Switch
18. External Stores Emergency Release
19. Cabin Air Temp Switch
20. Standby Compass
21. Optical Sight Unit
22. Radar Scope
23. True Airspeed Indicator
24. Fire Warning Light
25. Missile Status Panel
26. Missile Control Panel
27. Radar Altimeter
28. Airspeed and Machmeter
29. Angle-of-Attack Indicator
30. Accelerometer
31. Attitude Direction Indicator
32. Altimeter
33. Horizontal Situation Indicator
34. Vertical Velocity Indicator
35. Emergency Attitude Indicator
36. Navigation Function Selector Panel
37. Fuel Flow Indicator
38. Tachometers
39. Exhaust Gas Temp Indicators
40. Exhaust Nozzle Position Indicators
41. Multiple Weapons Control Panel
42. Oil Pressure Gauge
43. Control Column
44. Hydraulic Pressure Gauges
45. Elevon Trim Control
46. Gyro Erect Switch

F-104 STARFIGHTER

TAILORED SPECIFICALLY FOR THE AIR SUPERIORITY, BOMBER-INTERCEPTOR ROLE, THE INFAMOUS "MISSILE WITH A MAN IN IT" BECAME ONE OF THE COLD WAR'S FIRST MULTI-ROLE FIGHTERS.

As one of the first fighters capable of speeds in excess of Mach 2 to enter the USAF inventory, the F-104 was not embraced by the Americans. Success for the F-104 would be found abroad with the many NATO nations who used the fighter in both the fighter and tactical bomber role. The genesis of the F-104 originated during the Korean War. Clarence L. "Kelly" Johnson toured the theater asking F-86 and F-84 pilots what they would like to see in a future fighter. The response was for a fighter with much greater speed, increased rate of climb and a higher operational ceiling. Upon his return, Johnson was able to convince the USAF that it was time for a fighter that could replace the F-100 and was lighter, simpler and less costly. The USAF liked the idea and invited North American and Republic to submit proposals for a new lightweight fighter. On March 12, 1953, Lockheed won the contract for two prototypes designated XF-104. Just under a year later, the sleek, stubby-winged fighter was ready for its first flight.

The new XF-104 was in many ways a radical departure from existing fighter-design philosophy. Most if not all of the fighter's equipment was jammed into the fuselage, including all fuel tanks (later, wingtip fuel tanks were added) and a retractable undercarriage. The nose was sharply tapered and pointed, but the most distinct feature of the new fighter was its wings. Incredibly short in span, the leading edges were razor sharp and a danger to ground crew. On March 25, 1955, during test flights, the F-104 proved its worth with a blistering speed of Mach 1.79 (1,324 mph / 2,130 km/h).

Impressed with the results, the USAF ordered 17 YF-104As and 153 F-104As. Because of the fighter's high T-tail, the F-104 was equipped with a downward-firing ejection seat, which would cause a great deal of trouble and was later changed to an upward-firing ejection seat.

On January 26, 1958, the F-104 entered service with 83rd Interceptor Fighter Squadron near San Francisco, but was quickly grounded due to numerous turbojet engine malfunctions. Ironically, while this was happening, the F-104 shattered world speed and world altitude records on May 7 and 16, 1958 (1,404.19 mph / 2,259.83 km/h and 91,249 feet / 27,813 m). But these achievements were not enough. The USAF had reduced its procurement from a total of 722 to only 296. The USAF would eventually deploy only three squadrons of the F-104A and B model. A small number of the F-104C fighter-bomber variant were assigned to the 479th Tactical Fighter Wing, and saw service in Vietnam. The F-104 also saw combat during the 1965 war between Pakistan and India.

With the cuts made by the USAF, the F-104 program was threatened with extinction, but a sales coup by the Lockheed team turned the F-104 into an unprecedented global manufacturing success. Looking for a replacement for its aging F-84s, the German Luftwaffe choose the F-104G. The G model was an all-weather, multi-role attack fighter capable of carrying a 4,000-pound (1,815 kg) bomb-load. Other NATO nations followed suit, and the F-104 was built in Canada, Japan, Germany, Italy, the Netherlands and Belgium. The F-104 also flew with the air forces of Denmark, Norway, Spain, Turkey, Greece, Pakistan, Jordon and Taiwan, making it one of the most widely used Western fighters of the Cold War.

Above: In the 1960s, the CF-104 was used as a nuclear strike aircraft, and from 1971 on, it was used exclusively as a low-level attack aircraft. This CF-104 practices its craft by firing a salvo of CRV-7 air-to-ground rockets.
Right: The fastest aircraft to serve in the RCAF, the CF-104 was popularly known as "the missile with a man in it."

PILOT'S PERSPECTIVE
Colonel John David
RCAF (Ret.)

The CF-104 cockpit was quite large and very comfortable to operate in. It was designed for the pilot. Everything you needed was close to hand and extremely easy to reach. Ergonomically speaking, I think it was fairly well engineered.

My experience was with the CF-104G in the low-level nuclear strike and air-to-ground role. The workload in the CF-104G was unbelievably heavy when you were doing IFR (instrument flight rules) at speed and low level. You had to manage the cockpit, the radar, and the weapons control panel. But that was the beauty of the 104. The cockpit design. Certainly for the G model and the role it was designed for, it was really quite good.

The ground-mapping radar was an essential part of the cockpit, and the controls for it were well positioned on the left console just back of the throttle. One of the things that was a bit more difficult to manage was the special nuclear-weapons panel. There was a fairly sophisticated procedure that you had to go through in order to arm a special weapon and we were required to accomplish this at high speed, low level. You have to remember that you were in a single-seat cockpit flying 500 feet above ground and maybe lower, day and night in all weather, at 450 to 540 knots without terrain-following radar. There was tremendous pressure on you to fly an accurate altitude when flying IFR low level. We had auto-pilot, but I never used it on strike missions, as I never trusted the altitude hold mode at low level.

Forward visibility in the CF-104 was very good. Visibility for your six o'clock and looking back was poor. It wasn't anything like the F-86, or today's F-16/F-18.

I wouldn't have changed anything in the cockpit. I am not speaking for the A and B models, which were used primarily for air defense. For the roles that we used it in — reconnaissance, ground attack, nuclear strike and air defense augmentation — the only additional thing that I would have liked to have had was a radar altimeter.

It was a pilot's airplane. Under certain conditions it could be unforgiving, so you had to make sure you let it know who was flying the airplane. From a sophisticated cockpit point of view, it was light years ahead of its time when compared to the T-Bird and F-86 cockpits. Testimony to that is the fact that it was a very successful airplane for its era and the multiple roles it served.

LOCKHEED F-104C STARFIGHTER
USAF Museum, Dayton, Ohio

1. Auxiliary Trim Control Panel
2. TACAN Control Panel
3. Circuit Breakers
4. UHF Control Panel
5. Throttle
6. Standby Compass
7. Fire Warning Light
8. CIT Gauge
9. Remote Channel Indicator
10. Arresting Hook Release Button and Warning Light
11. External Stores Jettison Button
12. Landing Gear Control Switch
13. Landing Gear Lever
14. Landing and Taxi Light Switch
15. APC Cut-off Switch
16. Engine Anti-Ice Switch
17. Standby Attitude Indicator
18. Turn-and-Slip Indicator
19. Drag Chute Handle
20. Pylon Jettison Handle
21. Radar Lock-on Control
22. Landing Gear Position Lights
23. Gunsight Control Switches
24. Airspeed and Machmeter
25. Altimeter
26. Push-to-Erect Vertical Gyro Indicator
27. Landing Gear Release Handle
28. Wing Flap Position Indicators
29. Clock
30. Accelerometer
31. Rudder Pedal Adjustment Handle
32. Control Column
33. Bearing Distance Indicator
34. Course Indicator
35. Radar Scope
36. Armament Control Panel
37. Attitude Indicator
38. Vertical Velocity Indicator
39. Tachometer
40. Exhaust Gas Temp Indicator
41. Exhaust Nozzle Position Indicator
42. Ram Air Turbine Handle
43. Hydraulic Pressure Gauges
44. Face Plate Heat Rheostat
45. Canopy Jettison Handle
46. Fuel Flow Indicator
47. Oil Pressure Gauge
48. Cabin Altimeter
49. Oil Quantity Indicator
50. Emergency Nozzle Closure Handle
51. Automatic Pitch Control Indicator

REPUBLIC

F-105 THUNDERCHIEF

EARLY IN ITS CAREER THE F-105 WAS KNOWN AS THE LEAD SLED, ULTRA-HOG, AND THUNDERTHUD, BUT DURING THE VIETNAM WAR, THE THUNDERCHIEF WAS TRANSFORMED INTO THE FOREMOST FIGHTER-BOMBER OF THE WAR AND WAS AFFECTIONATELY KNOWN AS THE THUD.

On October 22, 1955, when the first YF-105A took to the air, it was the largest and heaviest single-seat single-engine fighter ever built. It was as long as the average World War II bomber and could carry both nuclear bombs and conventional stores over great distances. It was also the first tactical fighter-bomber to incorporate sophisticated electronic systems integrated to provide automatic navigation flight control and weapons delivery. The prototype reached an impressive Mach 1.2 with an engine with less power than the projected powerplant and a fuselage that had not been designed according to Area Rule principles. The second prototype, the YF-105B, powered by the right engine and redesigned fuselage, made its first flight on May 26, 1956. This aircraft reached an incredible Mach 2.15 — an amazing feat for a fighter of such size and weight. The F-105 was so large it was the only single-seat fighter to have a fully enclosed bomb bay. The Thunderchief could carry up to 8,000 pounds (3,630 kg) internally and a further 4,000 pounds (1,815 kg) externally. It was also equipped with a 20 mm M-61 Vulcan cannon with 1,029 rounds of ammunition on the left side of the nose.

In 1958 the F-105 was put into production. First off the line was the F-105B, of which 71 were built for the 4th Tactical Fighter Wing. Despite the aircraft's impressive performance, production was slow and it was not until June 1959 that the all-weather F-105D version took to the air. From 1960 to 1964, a total of 610 F-105Ds left the assembly lines. In late 1963, production switched to another variant, the F-105F trainer version (143 built), with full combat capability. Ironically, this two-cockpit, dual-control version saw as much if not more combat action in Vietnam than the single-seat variant. In 1966, 86 F-105Fs were converted to the F-105G Wild Weasel variant. This version was equipped with anti-radar systems and missiles capable of destroying surface-to-air (SAM) missiles sites.

War for the Thunderchief began on March 1, 1965. F-105s based at Da Nang flew their first bombing mission over North Vietnam.

The Thunderchief's task was not easy. The North Vietnamese air defenses were the most formidable in the history of aerial warfare. As a consequence, 350 Thunderchiefs were lost to missiles, fighters and anti-aircraft guns. While the F-105 was an excellent tactical bomber, its performance as a straight fighter was considerably lacking. Against the more nimble MiG-17s and MiG-21s, the "Thud" fared poorly, but in the end it did manage to shoot down 27 MiGs between 1966 and 1967.

When it first appeared, the F-105 Thunderchief was described as "the most powerful one-man airplane in the world." There were 824 F-105s built. They ended their days with the Air National Guard in 1984.

Above: Two F-105s on a bombing mission over South Vietnam, October 1968. Normal load for the Thunderchief was six 750-pound bombs on the fuselage centerline rack, with 450-gallon fuel tanks on the inboard wing sections. Right: A pilot climbs aboard his F-105. This example is from the 457th Tactical Fighter Squadron.

PILOT'S PERSPECTIVE
Colonel Clarence E. "Bud" Anderson
USAF (Ret.)

Some thirty years have transpired since I last flew the F-105D Thunderchief, during the later stages of the Vietnam War. In general I recall that the cockpit layout and instrumentation were quite adequate. I first flew the F-105 in October 1959. I was assigned to Edwards Air Force Base, California, as chief of the Flight Test Operations Division. There I conducted an evaluation flight on an F-105B model.

In 1965, I was assigned to the 18th Tactical Fighter Wing, which was located on Okinawa and equipped with the F-105D. The F-105D was the largest single-engine fighter ever built, and the cockpit was well planned and laid out. You could reach almost every switch and lever with ease. Some of the cockpit flight instruments were the vertical-tape type and different from the normal round gauges. These consisted of air-speed, Mach number, altitude and vertical-speed indicators. You adapted to the vertical tapes rapidly, and I don't recall any problems with interpretation. The idea was you could scan horizontally along one line back and forth, and that would reduce the workload.

The cockpit was comfortable and roomy, and the seat angle was comfortable, which was typical of most all Republic products. The rudder pedals had a wide range of adjustment so that almost everyone could easily get full rudder-control movement. The control stick was in the right place and your hand rested naturally on the grip. Switches and knobs seemed to all be in logical places. The weapons panel was fairly simple and user friendly, the knobs large and easy to operate.

The biggest objection I had to the cockpit arrangement was the canopy. It was small and in a clamshell arrangement. You could not turn your head and look to the rear very well, and I considered that a big deficiency in a fighter.

In 1970–71, I was the Commander of the 355th Tactical Fighter Wing in Thailand and had the opportunity to fly the F-105D in combat during the later stages of the Vietnam War. I have logged about 330 hours in F-105s.

REPUBLIC F-105G THUNDERCHIEF
USAF Museum, Dayton, Ohio

1. Flight Controls Panel
2. Command Radio Control Panel
3. Radar Control Panel
4. Bomb Toss Computer Control Panel
5. Throttle
6. Water Injection Switch
7. Burst Height Knob and Window
8. Landing Gear Emergency Extension Handle
9. Jettison External Stores Button
10. Landing Gear Handle
11. Anti-Skid Switch
12. Drag Chute Handle
13. Radar Warning Lights
14. Standby Airspeed Indicator
15. Remote Channel Indicator
16. Sight Control Panel
17. Standby Compass
18. Engine Overheat/ Fire Warning Panel
19. Airspeed-Mach Indicator
20. Standby Attitude Indicator
21. Fire Control Panel
22. Elevon Trim Control
23. Instrument Selector Switch
24. Dimmer Control Switch
25. Clearance Plane Indicator
26. Control Column
27. Attitude Director Indicator
28. Horizontal Situation Indicator
29. Radar Scope
30. Radar Control Panel
31. Armament Panel
32. Altitude-Vertical Velocity Indicator
33. Clock
34. Steer Needle Switch
35. Fuel Quantity Indicator
36. Antenna Tilt Indicator
37. Master Caution Light
38. Sight Radar Control Panel
39. Drift-Angle Ground Speed Indicator
40. Pressure Ratio Gauge
41. Exhaust Gas Temp Gauge
42. Fuel Flow Indicator
43. Fuel Quantity Selector Switch
44. Tachometer
45. Oil Pressure Gauge
46. Hydraulic Pressure Gauges
47. Anti-Skid Switch
48. Marker Beacon and High Toss Light
49. Standby Altimeter

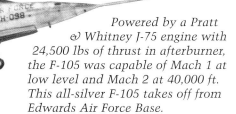

Powered by a Pratt & Whitney J-75 engine with 24,500 lbs of thrust in afterburner, the F-105 was capable of Mach 1 at low level and Mach 2 at 40,000 ft. This all-silver F-105 takes off from Edwards Air Force Base.

F-106 DELTA DART

CONSIDERED BY MANY EXPERTS THE BEST INTERCEPTOR EVER BUILT, THE F-106 PROVIDED THE USAF
WITH A ROBUST, DEPENDABLE AND FAST AIR-DEFENSE FIGHTER FOR OVER TWENTY-FIVE YEARS.

The history of the F-106 is tied directly to the development of the F-102 Delta Dagger, which entered service before the F-106 and was procured as a temporary stop-gap fighter until the F-106 was ready for service. On its maiden flight on October 24, 1953, the first F-102 failed to fly faster than the speed of sound. The second prototype also failed to reach the Mach 1 and caused much consternation among Convair's engineers. With Cold War tensions increasing, the need for an operational interceptor became a priority, and development of the advanced 106 was pushed aside in favor of the F-102. The delay in the F-106 program was partly due to problems with the J75 engine and the revolutionary MA-1 fire-control system.

The F-102 seemed doomed to failure, but happily a development at the laboratories of the National Advisory Committee for Aeronautics (now NASA) presented Convair with a way of reducing trans-sonic drag. The F-102 was quickly redesigned to take advantage of the new Area Rule developed by Richard T. Whitcomb. With the fuselage now shaped something like a Coke bottle, the F-102 slipped easily through the speed of sound. Deliveries of the new F-102 began in June 1955. As the new fighter reached squadron service, development of the more advanced F-106 continued. Designed along the same lines as the F-102, the F-106 incorporated the principles of the Area Rule from the outset and, souped up with an engine with 50 percent more power, the F-106 achieved a speed of Mach 1.9 and an altitude of 57,000 feet on its first flight.

By 1962, the Aerospace Defense Command (ADC) possessed 251 F-106A interceptors grouped in fourteen squadrons. The heart of the F-106 interceptor was the Hughes MA-1 fire-control system. Through a vast network of land-based radar, intercepting F-106s with the MA-1 system would automatically plot the intercept course, sight the target and fire the missiles. The F-106 performed this duty flawlessly and proved itself one of the world's best all-weather interceptors.

Throughout its operational life, the F-106 was continually updated with new and better equipment. In 1967, in-flight refueling was added, giving the F-106 longer legs and an ability to deploy overseas. Because of this increased, worldwide capability, the ADC realized that 106 pilots would have to prepare themselves for combat against enemy fighters. In the late 1960s, a program was launched to train 106 pilots in the fine art of air-to-air combat. In the process, the F-106 proved an excellent air-to-air fighter. Its large wing and high thrust showed the 106 to be superior to most of the USAF fighters in operation. The F-106 was also equipped with a Vulcan 20 mm cannon along with its four air-to-air missiles.

The F-106 did everything it was designed for and more. Entering service in 1959, the F-106 saw service in the United States, Alaska, Ireland, Canada and, for short spells, in Germany and South Korea. However, with the advent of the intercontinental ballistic missile, the days of the manned interceptor were numbered. After just 277 examples were built, the F-106 was canceled. The Air National Guard would fly the F-106 well into the mid-1980s.

Above: With drag chute deployed, an F-106 returns to Nellis Air Force Base, October 1971.
Right: An F-106 launches a Genie air-to-air missile during the William Tell 1972 gunnery competition.

PILOT'S PERSPECTIVE
Colonel Don Stevlingson
U.S. Air Force (Ret.)

When I got out of flight training I flew F-102s and then transferred to the F-106. I was one of the first guys to check out on the aircraft in my squadron. I flew the F-106 for eight years and logged about 3,000 hours. There was a big difference between the F-102 and F-106 cockpits. Although they looked similar, the F-106 was much more sophisticated. I remember looking into an F-102 cockpit after having flown the F-106 for a while and I thought, my God, there's nothing there. I thought the F-106 was the neatest thing in the world and, compared to the F-102, it was like a spaceship. The thing that was really impressive, initially, was the Tactical Situation Display that sat between your legs. When it worked, it would show your position on a moving map as well as your target's position. In the end it got so damn complex to maintain they started cutting those features out and the Tactical Situation Display became a great cockpit light.

I liked the size of the F-106 cockpit. It was big and comfortable and it was a wonderful airplane to go cross country. If you really wanted to stretch it out, you could take off from Montana and one-hop it all the way to D.C.

The environmental conditions in it were superb, but the one thing that was very uncomfortable was the oxygen regulator. You breathed 100-percent oxygen all the time under pressure. Basically you opened your mouth and let it fill your lungs. That system was hard to get used to and a lot of guys suffered horrible ear blocks after they landed.

The stick was different from other fighters. It had a control column that split into two. On the left you could control the radar and adjust your range gate while using your right hand to fly the airplane.

Visibility from the F-106 was not that good. Later modifications had a slightly bulged bubble-type canopy, but the visibility didn't improve that much.

Workload in the F-106 was really extreme. Running an intercept at night at low level, in a chaff, ECM environment was about as demanding as you could possibly get. The other interesting thing about the F-106 was that, of all the other interceptors in the U.S. inventory, it was the only aircraft that would have allowed a nuclear weapon to be put under the control of one person. All the other nuclear-capable interceptors were two-seaters.

CONVAIR F-106A DELTA DART
USAF Museum, Dayton, Ohio

1. Ram Air Turbine Handle
2. IFF/SIF Control Panel
3. Mask De-Fog Rheostat
4. Fuel Control Switch and Rudder Trim Switch
5. Frequency Selector Panel
6. Throttle
7. Armament Control Panel
8. Cockpit No-Fog Switch
9. Landing and Taxi Light Switch
10. ILS Channel Selector Panel
11. Master Electrical Power Switch
12. Idle Thrust Control Switch
13. Oxygen Control Panel
14. Landing Gear Audio Warning Button
15. Master Electrical Power Switch
16. External Wing Tanks Release Button
17. Landing Gear Control Panel
18. Radar Azimuth Control Panel
19. Landing Gear Control Handle
20. Landing Gear Emergency Release Handle
21. Radar Scope
22. Landing Gear Warning Light
23. Landing Gear Position Light
24. Drag Chute Handle
25. UHF Channel Selector
26. Clock
27. Flight Modes Panel
28. Heading Selector Switch
29. Computer Mode Indicator
30. Airspeed/Machmeter
31. Attitude Director Indicator
32. Bearing Selector Switch
33. Horizontal Situation Indicator
34. Vertical Velocity Indicator
35. Exhaust Gas Temp Gauge
36. Master Warning Light
37. Fuel Quantity Gauge
38. Hydraulic Pressure Warning Light
39. Fuel Flow Indicator
40. Radar Mode Panel
41. Tactical Situation Display
42. Control Stick
43. Standby Compass
44. Ejection Seat Handle

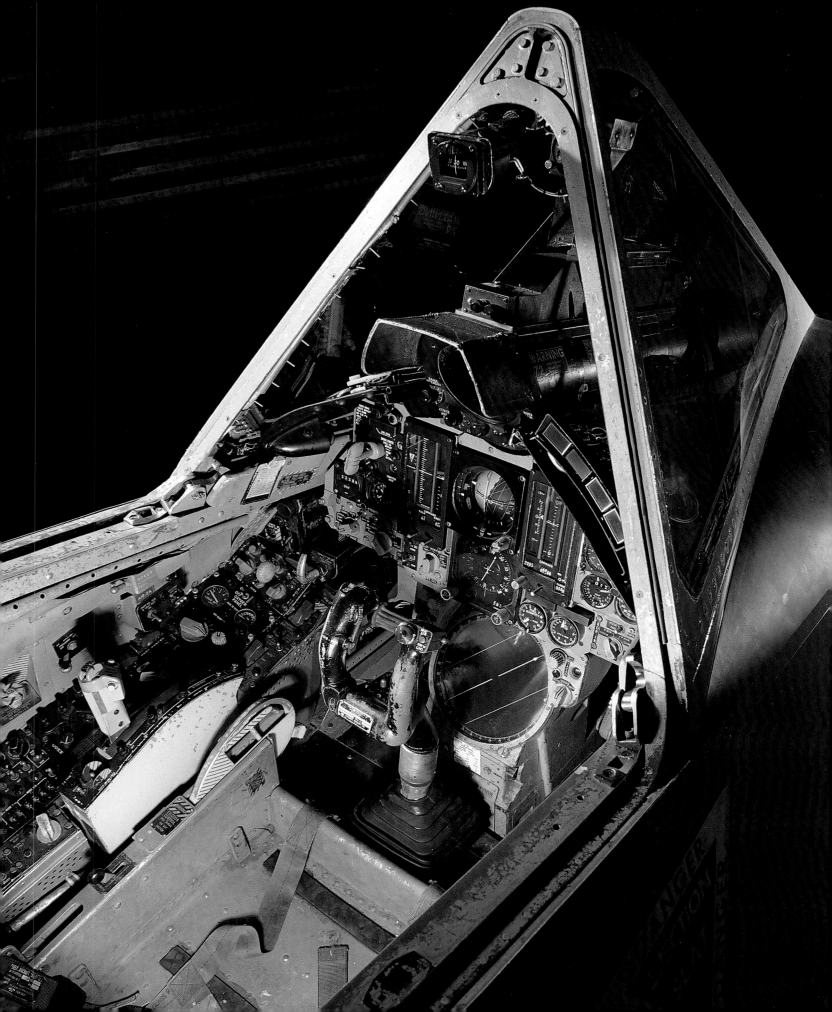

LOCKHEED

SR-71 BLACKBIRD

KNOWN AS THE SLED BY THE PILOTS WHO FLEW IT, THE SR-71 REMAINS
THE MOST IMPRESSIVE AND SECRETIVE COLD WAR AIRCRAFT TO THIS DAY.

In the late 1950s, the United States Air Force announced a design competition for a new reconnaissance aircraft capable of Mach 3 and able to operate at altitudes of 80,000 feet. This announcement, although made by the Air Force, had more to do with the CIA's request for a manned aircraft able to carry out photo-reconnaissance missions over enemy territory. General Dynamics, Boeing and North American submitted competing projects, but once again, Lockheed's

Kelly Johnson and his design team at "the Skunk Works" had just what the Air Force wanted.

On January 30, 1960, an order was placed for aircraft designated A-12. Two short years later, on April 26, 1962, Louis Schalk took off from a secret base known as "The Ranch" in the first A-12. Although not powered by the new J58 engines, the first A-12 showed great promise. When equipped with the new J58 engines, the A-12 proved itself and was immediately put into service by the CIA. The A-12 was soon turned into a high-altitude interceptor, the YF-12A. The YF-12A was fitted with fire-control radar and four Hughes Falcon missiles. The YF-12A was also the first Blackbird to be covered by a special black, thermally emissive paint. While a formidable interceptor, the new YF-12A would be impossible to fund, and the focus soon turned to strategic reconnaissance.

In December 1962, thirty-two SR-71s were ordered. These new aircraft had a greater overall length and were heavier than the A-12 and YF-12A. The airframes for A-12/YF-12A and SR-71 are 93 percent titanium and, amazingly, the component parts of the Blackbird are not a close fit — this deliberately so to allow the airframe to expand at high temperatures. At speeds of Mach 3, some sections of the aircraft can reach temperatures of 3,000 degrees Fahrenheit and the overall length of the aircraft can increase by 1 foot. Powered by two Pratt & Whitney J58 engines developing 32,500 pounds (14,740 kg) of thrust, the SR-71's powerplants are really two engines in one — a turbojet at low speeds and ramjet at speeds above 2,000 mph (3,220 km/h).

The ability of the SR-71 to reach sustained speeds of over Mach 3 and achieve altitudes up to 100,000 feet made it virtually untouchable. Flights over Cuba, China, North Korea and Vietnam were common during the Cold War. Attempts by the Soviets to shoot down the SR-71 came mostly from surface-to-air missiles (SAM) and not interceptors. The North Koreans and Cubans also fired off substantial numbers of SAMs at the high-flying Blackbirds. Although the SR-71 never "officially" flew over the USSR, it did skirt the borders and proved a major annoyance. In June 1986, the Soviets were finally able to mount a successful SR-71 intercept using their new MiG-31 Foxhounds. In a coordinated intercept over the Barents Sea, six MiG-31s subjected a lone SR-71 to an all-angle air-to-air missile intercept. Fortunately for the American crew, they were over international waters, but the Soviets had proved their point.

The SR-71 was finally retired in the early 1990s. Even today, three decades after its first flight, the Blackbird's capabilities remain unmatched.

Above: The SR-71 was the world's first truly "stealthy" aircraft. Designed to keep its radar cross-section as low as possible, it was also covered with a special paint that contained billions of microscopic iron balls that reduced radar reflectivity. Right: Dramatic in performance (Mach 3 above 85,000 feet), the SR-71 could monitor 100,000 miles in just one hour.

PILOT'S PERSPECTIVE
Colonel Richard Graham
USAF (Ret.)

I joined the SR-71 program in the summer of 1974. I got a lot of simulator time before I actually sat in the SR-71. When I did, I felt very much at home. The cockpit was quite comfortable. The pressure suit was more comfortable once you got used to it, and because you had to wear a suit, all the knobs and controls in the cockpit were oversized.

The stick control was very easy to handle. It was also oversized and designed to hold your pressure-suit hand. Everything was exaggerated on the stick grip in terms of push-to-talk buttons, air-refueling disconnect buttons and stuff like that.

Basically the only auto-pilot in the SR-71 was the auto-navigation system. Once you engaged the auto-nav, it would take over and navigate around the course automatically. We could hand-fly the SR-71, but you could never fly it smooth enough to get the high-quality imagery needed. Therefore we had a requirement that anytime the cameras and sensors were on, you had to have the auto-nav engaged.

The visibility from the SR-71, from inside the pressure suit, wasn't great. The windows were small. You could not see the wings at all. The one thing the SR-71 did have was a periscope. You could pop it up into the windstream and look back. Forward visibility was not great because the SR-71's cockpit was like the F-106's, with the tight, slanted windscreen. The windows were made of very thick, high-quality polished glass. The front windows at Mach 3 cruise would reach 700 degrees Fahrenheit. That's where I would warm up my squeeze-tube food.

Even though it was a very antiquated cockpit in terms of what most people think they're going to see, it was very well laid out. Everything was in a very functional area.

I flew the SR-71 for seven years. I also flew the U2. It was probably the most uncomfortable cockpit I ever experienced. It made the SR look ultra-modern.

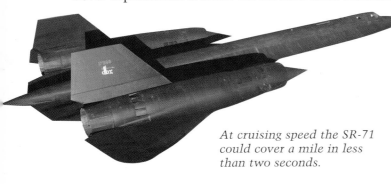

At cruising speed the SR-71 could cover a mile in less than two seconds.

LOCKHEED SR-71A BLACKBIRD
USAF Museum, Dayton, Ohio

1. UHF-1 Translator Panel
2. Canopy Jettison Handle
3. Throttle Quadrant
4. Rudder Pedal
5. Cockpit Light
6. Wet-Dry Switch
7. Brake Switch
8. Cockpit Temp Control and Override
9. Defog Switch
10. L Refrigeration Switch
11. R Refrigeration Switch
12. Temp Indicator Selector Switch
13. Temp Indicator
14. Drag Chute Handle
15. Compressor Inlet Temp Gauge
16. KEAS Warning Light
17. Air Refuel Switches
18. Angle-of-Attack Indicator
19. Standby Attitude Indicator
20. Airspeed/Machmeter
21. Egress Lights
22. Compressor Inlet Pressure Gauge
23. RSO Bailout Switch
24. APW Switch
25. Spike Position Indicator
26. Spike Controls
27. Inlet Restart Switches

28. Pitch Trim Indicator
29. Roll Trim Indicator
30. Yaw Trim Indicator
31. Forward Bypass Controls
32. Forward Bypass Position Indicator
33. Accelerometer
34. Triple Display Indicator
35. Attitude Director Indicator
36. Horizontal Situation Indicator
37. Elapsed Time Clock
38. Altimeter
39. Inertial-Lead Vertical Speed Indicator
40. Tachometers
41. Fire Warning Lights
42. Exhaust Gas Temp Indicators
43. Exhaust Nozzle Position Indicators
44. Fuel Flow Indicators
45. Oil Pressure Indicators
46. Hydraulic System Pressure Gauges
47. Fuel Quantity Indicator
48. Standby Liquid Nitrogen Gauge
49. Center of Gravity Indicator
50. Fuel Tank Pressure Gauge
51. Igniter-Purge Switch

52. Liquid Nitrogen Quantity Indicator
53. Fuel Boost Pump Switches
54. Manual Aft Transfer Switch
55. Forward Transfer Switch C
56. Canopy Seal Pressure Valve
57. Emergency Fuel Cut-off Switch
58. Fuel Dump Switch
59. Battery Switch
60. Emergency AC Bus Switch
61. Fuel Quantity Indicator Selector Switch
62. L & R Generator Switches
63. Generator Bus Tie Switch
64. Instrument Inverter Switch
65. SAS/Auto-pilot Control Panel
66. Interphone Control Panel
67. Navigation Map Indicator
68. Surface Limiter Release
69. Pitot Heat Switch
70. Windshield De-Icing Switch
71. Trim Power Switch
72. Emergency Gear Release
73. Ejection Seat Handle
74. Control Column

CONVAIR

B-36 PEACEMAKER

IN AVIATION TERMS, THE B-36 WAS A DINOSAUR. DIFFICULT TO MAINTAIN, EXPENSIVE TO FLY
AND FREQUENTLY IN NEED OF ENGINE CHANGES, THE B-36 WAS, DESPITE ITS INEFFICIENCIES, THE FIRST
COLD WAR BOMBER CAPABLE OF DELIVERING A NUCLEAR WEAPON DEEP INSIDE SOVIET TERRITORY.

The B-36 was conceived out of fear. The success of Nazi Germany over Britain in early 1940 was very real, and the shocking realization that the Germans just might succeed in conquering all of Europe led the United States to consider the need for an intercontinental bomber. A bomber of immense size was proposed, one capable of striking at Germany from the United States without refueling. It would become the biggest bomber ever built. Ten engines, a 230-foot (70 m) wingspan, and a crew of up to 22 would haul a bomb-load of 84,000 pounds (37,800 kg) to Europe and back (10,000 miles; 16,090 km).

Two manufacturers with big aircraft experience, Boeing and Consolidated (later to merge with Vultee to become Convair), received an invitation to bid for what many believed to be an impossible requirement. Two other companies entered the fray, Douglas and

Northrop, but they were unable to meet the range requirements. Boeing pressed ahead but felt the job was simply too big. It also had it hands full with the new B-29 Superfortress. Everything about the new bomber was big. So big, in fact, that many felt almost impossible to build, but as America's industrial might began to stir, engineering solutions for the new bomber began to emerge. In October 1941, Consolidated found a solution: a six-engined pusher design. In November, Consolidated was awarded a contract for two XB-36 prototypes. As the war progressed, however, the B-36 was put on a low priority. It was not until August 1946 that the XB-36 took to

Right: The B-36J was the last production version assigned to Strategic Air Command.
Above right: This B-36 belongs to the 4925th Test Group Atomic, used by the Special Weapons Command in connection with the Continental Nuclear Test Program in March 1953.

the air. While declared a success, it was clear it was not ready for production. The harsh lessons of the Second World War and the advent of the atomic bomb provided the impetus to keep the B-36 project moving forward.

Powered by six huge 3,000-horsepower Pratt & Whitney radial engines, the B-36 was slower than anticipated and its bombing altitude of 45,000 feet put it within easy reach of the new jet fighters. In order to boost performance, Convair mounted two podded General Electric (GE) Turbojet engines under each wing outboard of the six pusher engines. With the increased power, the B-36 could now reach 46,000 feet (14,020 m) with a dash speed of over 400 mph (645 km/h). Even with the increased speed,

the B-36 could not escape the thermal shock-wave created by an air-burst free-fall nuclear weapon bigger than 25 megatons.

The USAF received its first operational B-36A on June 26, 1948. Next in line was the B-36B, which carried the full complement of defensive armament of sixteen 20 mm cannon and was equipped to carry two massive 43,000-pound (19,520 kg) atomic bombs. Following service introduction, the B-36 fleet began to grow: 36 in 1949, 58 in 1950, 126 in 1951, 268 in 1952, 312 in 1953, with a peak of 342 in 1954. Once in service, the B-36 soon proved itself. In December 1948, a B-36 from the 7th Bomb Group flew nonstop from Texas to Hawaii and back.

PILOT'S PERSPECTIVE
Guy Townsend
USAF (Ret.)

The B-36 was one of the most unromantic aircraft I ever flew. In fact, you could get airsick just by being in it while still on the ground. With the outboard engines running, the plane would shake just like it was in rough air.

I flew the B-36 in flight test and flew the XB-36 back in 1946. Every time a new model came out, I'd go down and fly the airplane. That was from 1946 right through to 1951. The last model of the B-36, I consider the best of the bunch. It was a good airplane.

That cockpit on the XB-36 was buried in the airplane like in the B-29. It didn't have the bubble canopy. That was put on the second airplane. I was very satisfied with the cockpit originally. For those days and times, I thought the cockpit comfort level was quite adequate. I liked the roominess of the B-36 cockpit. I think Convair did a pretty good job. It wasn't a tremendous change going from the B-29 cockpit to the B-36. The B-36 had some unusual characteristics compared to the B-29, but it was a very easy airplane to fly. Like the B-29, the B-36 had a flight engineer, but in the B-36, because it had six pusher engines, the flight engineer had a primary position. Most B-36s flew with two flight engineers. There was so much damn stuff to watch back there.

The B-36 was not a hard airplane to fly and had very docile characteristics. You couldn't stall the airplane. The airplane was fixed from stalling. I don't think it bothered anybody, because the only time I stalled the airplane was when the number three propeller came off and crashed through the fuselage.

The auto-pilot in those days worked well, but compared to the auto-pilots of today, it was a bunch of junk. When we first started out with the B-36, it was very difficult to maintain. Everything broke. The ignition used to break down at high altitude, and the mechanics would install the spark plugs with surgical masks and white gloves to keep it as clean as possible.

The spec on the airplane was to go 10,000 miles, carry 100,000 pounds of bombs at 50,000 feet. It would do any one of these things, but not any two in the same mission.

CONVAIR B-36J PEACEMAKER
USAF Museum, Dayton, Ohio

1. Control Column
2. Flight Instrument Switches
3. Radio Magnetic Indicator
4. ARN-14 Course Indicator
5. Pilot's Data Indicator
6. Flap Position Indicator
7. Manifold Pressure Gauge
8. Propeller Reverse Warning Lights
9. Air-Speed Indicator
10. High Latitude Compass Repeater Indicator
11. Attitude Indicator
12. Master Tachometer
13. Jet Engine Tachometers
14. Turn-and-Bank Indicator

15. Aileron Trim Indicator
16. Jet Tail Pipe Temp Indicators
17. Throttles
18. Jet Fuel Pressure Gauges
19. Clock
20. Jet Oil Pressure Gauges
21. Throttle Lock Lever
22. Elevator Trim Tab Indicator
23. Master Motor Speed Control Lever
24. Elevator Trim Tab Wheel
25. Rudder Trim Tab Knob
26. Elevator Trim Tab Indicator
27. Turbo Boost Selector Lever
28. Aileron Trim Tab Switch

29. Bomb Bay Control Panel
30. Bomb Bay Door Volt Meter
31. Compass
32. Circuit Breakers
33. Throttle Lock Lever
34. Throttle Control Override Switches
35. Circuit Breakers
36. Oil Shut-off Valve Switches
37. Throttles
38. Throttle Control Selector Switches
39. Fuel Valve Indicator Lamps
40. Circuit Breaker Panel
41. Engine Fuel Valve Switches
42. Engine Starter Switches
43. Ignition Start Switches
44. Panel Lights Switch

BOEING
B-47 STRATOJET

Exceptionally bold in concept, the B-47 shattered any preconceived notions of what a bomber should look like. Its fighter-type cockpit and thin, swept surfaces were a dramatic leap forward and shaped the design of future military and civilian aircraft.

Through the 1950s and early 1960s, Boeing's B-47 Stratojet was the backbone of the U.S. Strategic Air Command. Like the contemporary F-86 Sabre, the B-47 owed much of its success to German wartime research into swept-back wing design. Work on the new jet bomber began in 1943. With a swept-back wing of 35 degrees, and six turbojets in underwing pods, the B-47 was an incredible marriage of sleek aerodynamics and raw jet power. The Air Force was impressed with Boeing's design and ordered two prototypes in May 1946. The first prototype flew on December 17, 1947, with six 3,750-pound-thrust (1,705 kg) General Electric J35 jet engines. Less than a year later, this aircraft flew a record-breaking flight of 2,289 miles in 3 hours, 46 minutes — an average speed of 607.8 mph (3,683 km; 977 km/h).

Production of the B-47 began in September 1948. Ten pre-production B-47As were built and the first flew on June 25, 1950. The first B-47 ready for squadron service was the B model; it flew for the first time in April 1951. Very different from the A model, the B-47 now had two auxiliary fuel tanks beneath the wings, in-flight refueling capability, more powerful engines and two .50-caliber machine guns in the tail. A total of 418 B-47Bs were built, 399 by Boeing, 10 by Douglas and 9 by Lockheed.

In mid-1951, the 306th (Medium) Bomb Wing was the first to receive their new mount. Like all new air-craft of such an advanced design, the B-47 had its share of problems. The thin wing of the B-47 flexed as much as 17 feet at its tip, and under turbulent conditions it

tended to act as an aileron. B-47 pilots also coined the phrase "the coffin corner" while flying the new bomber. This was the altitude at which the airspeed for low-speed and compressibility stalls coincided. But the B-47's principal limitation was its range on internal fuel — only 1,500 miles (2,415 km). Once again, Boeing had an answer to the problem. Even before the first B-47 wing was formed, the 306th Air Refueling Squadron took delivery of the KC-97 tanker. This made the B-47 a true intercontinental bomber — and meant that every B-47 Wing it had to be supported by a squadron of twenty KC-97 tankers.

In 1952, the B-47B was succeeded by the E model. This proved to be the definitive version and was built in greater numbers (1,359) than any other model. The new E variant was equipped with six General Electric J47 engines with 6,000-pound (2,730 kg) thrust, a new radar-directed tail barbette housing two 20 mm cannon and ejection seats for the three crew members. In 1957, the Strategic Air Command reached a peak strength of 1,800 B-47 Stratojets. As remarkable as the B-47 was, it was however, just an intermediate step in SAC's long-term plan. What the B-47 had proven, the remarkable Boeing B-52 would incorporate into a truly fearsome bomber. In 1955, SAC began to take delivery of their new bomber and the B-47 was slowly phased out. Incredibly, in September 1964, there were still 500 B-47s of all types in USAF service equipping nine SAC Wings. In 1969, the last B-47E flew for the Military Airlift Command. A total of 2,042 B-47s were built.

Above: The B-47 was the first swept-wing bomber to attain quantity production and was built in larger numbers than any other Western strategic aircraft. Right: Ground crew of a B-47 from the 310th Bomb Wing check over their aircraft at McCoy Air Force Base, October 1959.

PILOT'S PERSPECTIVE
Colonel Dick Purdum
USAF (Ret.)

When the B-47 first came out there wasn't a fighter that could keep up with it. For example, if we had F-86s making runs against us we could run away from them.

I flew the B-47 for over ten years and have 3,900 hours flying time in the B-47. I went from pilot training right into the co-pilot seat of the B-47. When you were coming out of a single-engine jet like the T-33, the B-47 cockpit was just absolutely awesome. The basic cockpit was not that much different from the T-33. The B-47 had a tandem cockpit like the T-33, with the pilot in front and the co-pilot in the back under a big bubble canopy. The B-47 had a three-man crew with a navigator/bombardier in the nose with a downward ejection seat and the pilots had upward ejection.

The B-47 was a very busy airplane to fly. There were times when I went out on an eight-hour mission and never had an opportunity to open my flight lunch. By comparison, the three people in the B-47 did basically what six people did in the B-52. Crew coordination in the B-47 was super critical. You could not see what the co-pilot was doing, so you had to really follow the checklist religiously and always get a response from the other crew member to insure that he had accomplished his required task as on the checklist.

The comfort level in the B-47 was terrible. Of course, there's no place to stand up in the airplane. The seat was not as comfortable as the seat in a B-52, not that the B-52 ejection seat was that comfortable. I would say 80 percent of people who flew the B-47 or even the B-52 have lower back problems. During daylight missions you'd boil because the canopy acted like a greenhouse. To make it halfway comfortable for the pilot meant the navigator/bombardier froze in the front. Fortunately most of our missions were at night. The visibility from the B-47 was outstanding and the canopy was probably three feet wide, which made for a roomy cockpit.

The cockpit was pretty well designed. I guess the only bad thing was when you had to reach down to the left in the co-pilot's position to reset the radios. You could easily get vertigo during a night flight or in bad weather as you reached down and turned you head to the left to reset your frequency.

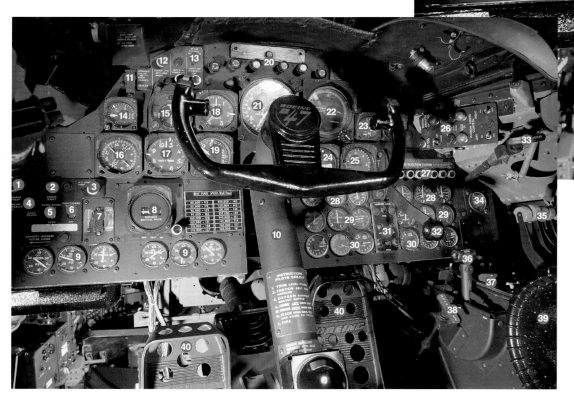

BOEING RB-47H STRATOJET
USAF Museum, Dayton, Ohio

1. Empenage Overheat Warning Light
2. Bombs Away Indicator Light
3. N-1 Compass Inoperative Light
4. Bomb Doors Position Indicator
5. Alternate Bomb Door Switch
6. Directional Damper Switch
7. Readiness Switch
8. Distance Indicator
9. Oil Pressure Gauges
10. Control Column
11. Approach Chute Switch
12. Anti-Skid Inoperative Light
13. ID Course Selector Switch
14. Accelerometer
15. ID-249
16. ID-250 Radio Compass
17. Machmeter
18. Airspeed Indicator
19. Altimeter
20. Fire Shutoff Switches
21. Directional Indicator
22. Attitude Indicator
23. Wing Flap Position Indicator
24. Turn-and-Slip Indicator
25. Vertical Velocity Indicator
26. Surface Power Control Panel
27. Water Injection Indicator Lights
28. Tachometers
29. Engine Fuel Flowmeters
30. Exhaust Gas Temp Gauges
31. Landing Gear Position Indicators
32. Landing Gear Lever
33. Brake Chute Deployment Handle
34. Outside Air Temp Gauge
35. Throttles
36. Steering Ratio Selector Lever
37. Exterior Surfaces Anti-Icing Switch
38. Parking Brake Handle
39. Elevator Trim Control
40. Rudder Pedals

73

BOEING

B-52 STRATOFORTRESS

COLD WAR HEAVYWEIGHT AND STILL THE CHAMPION — THE REMARKABLE B-52
HAS SYMBOLIZED U.S. STRATEGIC AIR POWER FOR MORE THAN FOUR AND A HALF DECADES
AND IS THE LONGEST-LIVED COMBAT AIRCRAFT DESIGN EVER PRODUCED.

In 1946, Boeing began work on a very large bomber with immense range. At first the new bomber was a stretched version of the B-29 with six engines, but by 1948 the design had changed to include four turboprop engines mounted on swept-back wings. This design did not meet the performance requirements of the USAF, and it was not until the introduction of the Pratt & Whitney J57 high-compression turbojet that the B-52 met the USAF's speed and range specifications. Powered by eight J57 engines hung in four underwing pods, the new B-52 had an unfueled range of well over 4,000 miles (6,400 km). The first flight of the B-52 occurred on April 15, 1952. It was followed by the first production model, the B-52A, which rolled off the production line in March 1954. Only three B-52As were produced, and all were used for test and development work. Next in line were fifty B models, which were delivered to the Strategic Air Command's (SAC) 93rd Bomb Wing at Castle Air Force Base, California, in June 1955. The B-25B was followed by the C model, which was essentially the same as the B but carried an additional 41,700 gallons (189,570 L) of fuel. In May of 1955 the D model emerged. There were 170 Ds built, and all B-52D were later modified and given the "big belly," which increased its conventional bomb-carrying capability to eighty-four 500-pound (1,100 kg) bombs.

It was not long before SAC showed the world what the B-52 was truly capable of. In January 1957, three B-52s of the 93rd Bomb Wing, supported by KC-97 tankers, flew from California, via Labrador, Morocco, Ceylon, the Philippines, Guam, and Hawaii, nonstop around the world. They covered 24,325 miles (39,140 km) in just 45 hours and 19 minutes! In October 1957 the B-52E appeared. This variant carried improved navigation and electronics and was equipped with the new AGM-28 Hound Dog supersonic nuclear stand-off missile. The biggest single change in design came with the B-52G model. First flown in October 1958, it was the first B-52 to have a "wet" wing, which increased fuel capacity by 16,000 gallons (72,735 L) The last B-52 variant to leave the production line was the H model. Equipped with new engines, the H had an unrefueled range of 12,500 miles (20,000 km), 2,500 miles (4,000 km) more than the G. A total of 102 H models were built.

During the Vietnam War, the B-52 was used extensively in both the tactical and the strategic role. Used first in the tactical role, the B-52 was called upon to support the ground troops. B-52Fs carrying twenty-seven 750-pound (1,650 kg) bombs internally and twenty-four more on external racks were tasked with bombing missions under the code name Arch Light.

In 1991, during the Gulf War, the B-52 saw action once again. Flying from bases in the Indian Ocean, the United Kingdom, Spain and Saudi Arabia, they were used in saturation bombing of soft targets, particularly Republican Guards units in the desert.

Today the B-52 continues to provide valuable service with the USAF in its efforts to destroy the Taliban and al Qaeda terrorist units in Afghanistan. Both the G and H model are expected to serve for at least one more decade. In total, 742 B-52s were built.

The B-52 could carry a wide variety of free-fall and stand-off nuclear weapons. This B-52H is armed with four Skybolt missiles. The Skybolt was never adapted by SAC and the program was canceled in 1962.

PILOT'S PERSPECTIVE
Colonel Chuck Anderson
USAF (Ret.)

I was in flight test at Wright Field when I was picked as the B-52 project pilot in 1955. I flew the tandem XB and YB-52. In fact, I spent so much time at Boeing, I flew the first fifteen B-52s ever built.

I thought the tandem cockpit arrangement in the XB and YB-52 was the worst crew configuration they could have had. There was no real coordination between you and the co-pilot. When they finally changed to the side-by-side configuration, I was quite impressed. After the flight-test work with Boeing, I went into SAC (Strategic Air Command). I'm indebted to SAC for one thing — they gave me the incentive to retire. As an example, when I first started flying the B-52, the pilot's checklist was on one side of a five-by-seven card, the co-pilot's was on the other. In SAC, if I remember correctly, the normal checklist was forty-two pages!

The visibility from the B-52 was normal for a big airplane. The only thing I didn't like was the oil pressure gauges. They were above the windshield, and I hardly ever looked at them. Other than that, I thought the instruments were fairly well grouped.

The B-52 cockpit was very comfortable. The workload was distributed almost equally throughout the cockpit. As for the flight-control system,

Boeing overreacted after the B-47. The B-47 had a fully powered hydraulic flight system. Later they realized that if you got a strike during combat and it severed a hydraulic line, you could lose the flight controls. The only thing that was power-controlled in the B-52 was the spoilers, which augmented the ailerons and the stabilizer trim. Both of those inputs had to be manually conducted, and with the stick forces being about 37 pounds, that was a lot of work.

I flew many 24-hour "chrome dome" missions. On each mission we would make two in-flight refuelings. It would take 25 to 28 minutes without a disconnect. When it was over, you were exhausted. I set up a system with my co-pilot where I'd make contact with the tanker and then he would put his hand on top of my throttle hand. I would then slide my hand off from underneath and then he'd handle the power. That made it a lot easier.

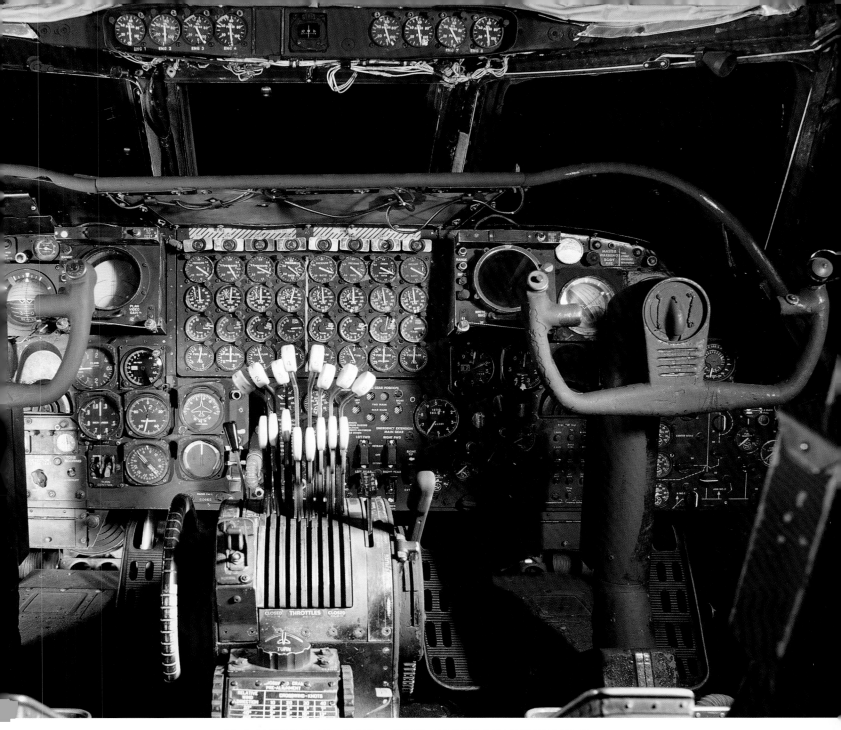

BOEING B-52D STRATOFORTRESS
USAF Museum, Dayton, Ohio

1. Trim Control
2. Intercom Switch
3. Mach Indicator Switch
4. Flight Command Indicator
5. Automatic Pilot Disengaged Light
6. Hydraulic Pack Pressure Low Master Light
7. Clearance Plane Indicator
8. Attitude-Director Indicator
9. Terrain Display Indicator
10. Vertical Velocity Indicator

11. Rudder Pedals
12. Control Column
13. Engine Fire Detector System Test Switch
14. Aileron Trim Indicator
15. Tone Scoring Interrupt Switch
16. Mach Indicator
17. Radar Altimeter
18. True Airspeed Indicator
19. Auto-pilot Turn Control Selector Switch

20. Radio Magnetic Indicator
21. Airbreak Lever
22. Stabilizer Trim Wheels and Indicators
23. Stabilizer Trim Cutout Switch
24. Crosswind Crab Control Knob
25. Engine-Pressure Ratio Gauges
26. Tachometers
27. Exhaust Gas Temperature Gauges

28. Fuel Flowmeters
29. Heading Indicator (Gyro)
30. Lateral Error Meter
31. Landing Gear Control
32. Throttles
33. Engine Fire Warning Lights/Firewall Fuel Shutoff Switches
34. Time-to-Go Light
35. Oil Pressure Gauges
36. Magnetic Standby Compass

37. Landing Gear Controls
38. Throttle Break Lever
39. Drag Chute Lever
40. Total Fuel Flow Indicator
41. Fuel System Controls
42. Altimeter
43. Airspeed Indicator
44. Master Fuselage Overheat (Fire) Warning Light
45. Gunner's Cabin Pressure Warning Light

GRUMMAN
F9F PANTHER

On July 3, 1950, F9F Panthers from the USS Valley Forge shot down two Yak-9s. From then on, Grumman's first jet fighter played a major role in the Cold War's first hot skirmish.

The F9F began life as a two-seat carrier-based night fighter. At the time the only turbojet available was the Westinghouse J30, which produced only 1,500 pounds (680 kg) of thrust. A multiple-engine design was considered, but this was dropped in favor of a single-seat, single-engine configuration using a British Rolls-Royce Nene engine. Two prototypes were ordered, one powered by the 5,000-pound (2,270 kg) British Nene engine and the other powered by the 4,600-pound (2,090 kg) Allison J33.

On November 24, 1947, the Nene-powered XF9F-2 prototype made its maiden flight. A year later the Allison-powered XF9F-3 took to the air. The Allison-powered XF9F-3 did not perform as well as the XF9F-2, and subsequently all F9F-3 were produced as F9F-2s, powered by the license-built Pratt & Whitney Nene engine. A total of 621 F9F-2s were produced before switching to the series 5 version. The F9F-5 had a stretched fuselage and higher tail assembly. The F9F-2/5 series aircraft had a tricycle landing gear and a pressurized cockpit with bubble canopy, and all series aircraft were fitted with auxiliary fuel tanks located under the wingtips.

When the Korean War broke out, Grumman was once again front and center with a rugged and reliable carrier fighter. Navy Panther squadrons bore the brunt of the fighting and chalked up their first victories with two Yak-9s shot down in July 1950. On November 9, 1950, Lieutenant Commander W. T. Amen, commanding officer of VF-11, scored the first MiG-15 kill by a carrier-based jet in an F9F-2. The Marines soon entered the fray, with VMF-331 flying its first Korean missions in F9F-2s. While the Marines were using the Panther as a fighter-bomber, the first Navy bombing missions were not flown until April 1951. From then on, Navy and Marine Panthers operated primarily in the fighter-bomber role. Grumman's traditional ruggedness came through once again and many damaged F9Fs made it back to fight another day. The F9F also had the honor of being the first jet fighter to equip the famous Blue Angels. In the summer of 1949, F9F-2s joined the display team only to be disbanded in the early weeks of the Korean War. In 1952, they reformed on the F9F-5, equipped with the more powerful Pratt & Whitney J48 engine developing 7,250 pounds (3,290 kg) of static thrust. The last F9Fs were taken out of service in 1957 and, like most typical Navy combat types, the Panther took over the role of advanced trainer. The only foreign customer for the F9F was the Argentine Navy, which obtained a small number in the late 1950s. As more advanced swept-wing fighters joined the fleet, the F9F-2 and 5s were moved into non-combat squadrons. The Marines were the last to maintain full combat squadrons of Panthers; VMA-223 and VMF(AW)-314 had F9F-5s as late as October and December 1957. The rugged F9F Panther served the U.S. Navy well and continued in service with advanced training command and the reserves into the early 1960s.

Like the all the other big cats that came before the F9F, the Grumman Panther proved an excellent multi-role aircraft and was immensely popular with the men who flew it.

Left: A Grumman F9F-5 from VF-154 lowering its wings in preparation for take-off. Above: The swept-wing version of the Panther was the F9F-6/8 Cougar. With the new wing and more powerful engine, the Cougar was 85 mph (137 km/h) faster. Cougars were standard equipment for the majority of the Navy's carrier-based fighters and used by the Blue Angels until 1958.

PILOT'S PERSPECTIVE
Robert L. Rasmussen
U.S. Navy (Ret.)

I first flew the F9F in 1953 when I joined Fighter Squadron 51, which was returning from a combat deployment in the Korean War. I checked out in their combat birds, the F9F-5 Panther, before the squadron switched to the F9F-6 Cougar, a swept-wing version of the Panther.

I was frankly a little disappointed with the Panther and Cougar cockpits. The only other jet I had flown at that time was the TV. It was a very compact, slim, accessible cockpit and everything looked like it was in the right place. I was pretty much of a novice, but that's the way I felt about the TV-1 and TV-2 (Navy versions of the P-80 and T-33). I can remember having the feeling that the F9F cockpit was just too roomy, giving the feeling of sitting in the aircraft as opposed to strapping it on and being part of the machine. Despite over a thousand hours flying the F9, I never got the feeling that I was part of the airplane — a difficult thing to define but very significant for a pilot of a fighter plane. That notwithstanding, I liked the Grumman products a lot. They're strong and reliable.

The comfort level in the F9 was good in part because of all of the room. Grumman birds were then built sort of like barrels — wide and round — mostly because of the large-diameter centrifugal-flow engine, which in turn dictated a wide fuselage, and that was reflected in the cockpit. The air conditioning was good; the controls were easy to handle and reach. The visibility was good, but not perfect. There was a sense that the structure of the cockpit submerged the pilot to the neck in airplane, limiting visibility to the side and aft.

The workload in the cockpit was relatively light, mainly because the aircraft was pretty simple. I would compare it to the F6F Hellcat in terms of what the pilot had to do to effectively operate the aircraft. There were a few things about the cockpit that were inconvenient. The wing-fold mechanism was a little difficult, but that's common in any navy airplane. It was necessary to take a couple of overt actions to get the wings folded, for good reason. On the first carrier landing I made in the F9F, I yanked to a stop and was given a wing-fold signal by the flight deck director. I could not find the handle and was afraid to take my eyes off the director to look. Finally, after an embarrassing delay, the director gave me a signal all carrier pilots would like to avoid: Pull your head out and look around. I made it a point to learn where the handle was.

GRUMMAN F9F-6 COUGAR
National Museum of Naval Aviation, Pensacola, Florida

1. Ejection Seat Pre-ejection Lever
2. Elevator Trim Tab Position Indicator
3. Rudder Trim Tab Control
4. Gun Ranging Radar Control
5. Stabilizer Control Selection Panel
6. Control Column
7. Wingtip Fuel Control Panel
8. Wing Flaps Control
9. Rudder Pedal
10. Air Conditioning Controls
11. Engine Control Switch Panel
12. Elevator Trim Tab Control Switch
13. Gun Button
14. Throttle with Microphone Button
15. Oxygen Regulator
16. Landing Gear Control Lever
17. Canopy Control
18. Landing Gear Emergency "T" Handle
19. Landing Gear Down Lock Solenoid Emergency Manual Release
20. Armament Switch Panel
21. Radio Altimeter Low Limit Light
22. Low Fuel Boost Pressure Warning Light
23. Oil Pressure Warning Light
24. Radio Altimeter
25. Oil Pressure Indicator
26. Wheels and Flaps Position Indicator
27. Gunsight
28. Tachometer
29. Tailpipe Temp Indicator
30. Airspeed Indicator
31. Altimeter
32. Remote Compass Indicator
33. Turn-and-Bank Indicator
34. Gyro Horizon
35. Rate-of-Climb Indicator
36. Fuel Gauge
37. Radio Compass
38. Clock
39. Standby Gyro Horizon
40. Take-off Check List
41. Standby Compass
42. Location of Stop Clock
43. Accelerometer
44. Fire Warning Light
45. Fuel Quantity Gauge Press-to-Test Button
46. Fire Warning Light
47. Fire Warning Light
48. Fire Warning Circuit Test Switch
49. Fuel Level Warning Light
50. Seat Height Control
51. Hydraulic Emergency Auxiliary Pump Switch
52. Radio Control Panel
53. Rocket and Bomb Firing Trigger

DOUGLAS

F4D SKYRAY

"THE TEN-MINUTE KILLER" WAS THE U.S. NAVY'S FIRST SUPERSONIC FIGHTER
AND IS IRONICALLY BEST REMEMBERED FOR ITS EXCELLENT DOGFIGHTING CAPABILITIES.

In 1947, the U.S. Navy issued a request for a short-range, carrier-based delta-wing interceptor fighter, capable of shooting down an enemy aircraft at 50,000 feet within five minutes of the first alarm bell.

After the Second World War, both Douglas and the Navy were anxious to exploit German research in regards to the delta-wing platform. By 1948, an order was placed for two prototypes, designated XF4D-1. The new aircraft came with a short tricycle landing gear, unusual among high-performance carrier-based jets of that time, and the wing was not a delta planform but a thin, cantilever mid-wing with rounded tips. There were no horizontal tailplanes, only elevons on the wing's trailing edge. An ejection seat was fitted and the cockpit was located well forward in the nose, which contained the Aero 13 system, including the APQ-50A radar. The Skyray was armed with four 20 mm cannons located in the wings. Designed around the 11,600-pound-thrust (5,260 kg) Westinghouse XJ40-WE-8 engine with afterburner, the Skyray would not enter service with this engine.

The first flight of the XF4D-1 took place on January 23, 1951, with test pilot Larry Peyton at the controls. At the beginning of the flight, Peyton had his hands full: during the initial climb out, the control stick had to be pushed fully forward right against the instrument panel in order to avoid a stall. The powerful effects of the longitudinal trimmers had not been fully appreciated at the time. After sorting out the problems, Peyton successfully landed the new prototype. Apart from the early difficulties, the XF4D-1 handled well, leading to

an order for the first twelve. By this time, the Navy had lost confidence with the Westinghouse J40 engine and opted for the Pratt & Whitney J57-P-8, which had the required thrust (10,200 pounds; 4,635 kg), but was a much larger engine. Because of this, 80 percent of the airframe had to be modified — because of the resulting further delays to the program, deliveries were not made to front-line squadrons until 1956!

Only one F4D was powered by the Westinghouse J40, and it set a new world record over one mile at 752.944 mph (3 km at 1,211.487 km/h) on October 3, 1953. But despite the problems with the installation of the J57 powerplant, the F4D-1 easily exceeded the speed of sound, and on May 22 and 23, 1958, Major N. Le Faivre shattered five world climb-to-height records, reaching 49,221 feet in 2 minutes, 36 seconds. In 1956, the F4D finally began to enter squadron service and became the U.S. Navy's first supersonic fighter. In total, 419 F4Ds were built and they served with twelve U.S. Navy squadrons and eight USMC squadrons.

During its front-line service, the Skyray proved popular with its pilots and was not only an excellent interceptor, but proved useful as a close-support aircraft. Because of its outstanding rate of climb and armed with four 20 mm cannon and Sidewinder missiles, the F4D-1 was also used as part of the USAF's air defense of North America. In 1961 the Skyrays began their transfer to Reserves and Utility Squadrons. The last front-line fleet aircraft were turned in by VMF-115 in 1964. The last unit to fly the Skyray was the U.S. Navy Test Pilot School, which used the aircraft until 1971.

Left: Four Skyrays in formation from the carrier USS Forrestal. Above: Deck space on an aircraft carrier is always in short supply. With wings folded, an F4D-1 from VF-141 is towed to its parking spot.

PILOT'S PERSPECTIVE
Lieutenant Colonel Hap Langstaff
USMC (Ret.)

I first flew the F4D in 1957. I was in command of a F9F Panther Squadron when they came looking for someone to take command of VMF-115 equipped with the F4D Skyray. Before that I flew about forty-one different aircraft in my career, including the Wildcat and Corsair on Guadalcanal.

When I first sat in the F4D cockpit, it was kind of overwhelming because it was larger then the F9F and you had an afterburner. The starting technique, armament and landing-gear controls were all a little different as well. The F4D was an all-weather interceptor designed to fire the Sidewinder missile. That meant the instrumentation was quite a bit different, compared to the Grumman F9F. It was probably the most modern cockpit I experienced and it was the last fighter I flew before I retired.

It was a comfortable cockpit. I'm very small in stature, and this was a big man's aircraft. The F4D's cockpit was fairly large and very convenient. I didn't have any trouble in the cockpit. The controls and instruments were very close and easy to reach. The starting technique with the afterburner turned out to be pretty tricky. You had to be careful with that, but overall I thought it was well organized.

Visibility from the F4D was excellent. The seat adjustment was such that you could put the seat into a good position so you could see well to both sides and to the rear. The lighting in the cockpit was good as well.

The workload on the F4D cockpit was heavy. With the radar being your key item, your concentration was focused on trying to find your contact and then locking on. Of course, you also had to fly the aircraft and that meant looking at your gauges at the same time! It was especially tricky at night when you fired a Sidewinder.

If I could have changed anything in the F4D cockpit, I would have added a radar screen. That would have been ideal. Everything would have been centrally located. You wouldn't have had to look right or left down into the cockpit. Everything you needed to know would have been on a screen right in front of you.

With that big bat wing, the Skyray was easy to control. In afterburner and moving through the speed of sound, you hardly even noticed — it was that stable.

DOUGLAS F4D-1 SKYRAY
National Museum of Naval Aviation, Pensacola, Florida

1. Canopy Latch Handle
2. Radar Control Panel
3. Pitch Trim Motor Circuit Breaker
4. Auto Control Panel
5. Throttle
6. Rudder Trim Control Knob
7. Throttle Friction Control Lever
8. Drop Tank Release Handle

9. Yaw Damper and Auto-pilot Switch
10. Fuel System Control Switch
11. Release Handle
12. Liquid Oxygen Indicator
13. Cabin Pressure Altimeter
14. Emergency Canopy Jettison
15. Emergency Landing Gear Lower Handle
16. Inverter Failure and Boost Pump Warning Lights

17. Trim Position Advantage Indicator
18. Pressure Ratio Indicator
19. Landing Gear Handle
20. Angle-of-Attack Indicator
21. APN-22 Height Indicator
22. Tachometer
23. Oil Pump Failure Warning Light
24. Airspeed Indicator

25. Altimeter
26. Tailpipe Temp Indicator
27. Elevon Hydraulic Pressure Indicator
28. Control Stick
29. ID-250/ARN Course Indicator
30. Turn-and-Bank Indicator
31. Gyro Horizon Indicator
32. Rate-of-Climb Indicator

33. Utility Hydraulic Pressure Indicator
34. UHF Remote Channel Indicator
35. ID-249/ARN Course Indicator
36. Fuel Flowmeter
37. Fuel Quantity Main Tanks
38. Accelerometer
39. Fuel Quantity Test Gauge
40. Ejection Seat Handle

GRUMMAN
F11 TIGER

THE FIRST FIGHTER TO BENEFIT FROM THE AREA RULE-DESIGNED FUSELAGE WAS NOT THE F-102 DELTA DAGGER, BUT THE GRUMMAN F11 TIGER, WHICH PRECEDED YF-102 BY SEVERAL MONTHS.

On April 27, 1953, the Grumman Aircraft Corporation received yet another order for a new fighter. Three prototypes were ordered for a carrier-based fighter capable of sustained supersonic speeds. What started out as a more advanced version of the F9F-6 Cougar quickly changed into something completely different. The aircraft that was to emerge bore no resemblance to the Cougar. The Grumman design team headed by Joseph Gavin used the new Area Rule principle (see the Convair F-106 Delta Dagger) to completely redesign the fuselage.

As a result, the air inlets for the jet engines had been moved from the wing root to a lateral position in the fuselage. The swept wing was much thinner and mounted as a midwing. It also incorporated leading-edge slats and ailerons across the entire span of the trailing edge. Because of this, only the wingtips could be folded. With the mid-wing design, the landing gear no longer retracted into the wings as in the F9F, but into the fuselage. Using the same design philosophy that went into the very successful F8F Bearcat, the Grumman design team wanted to create a small, lightweight fighter powered by the most powerful and reliable engine available.

On July 30, 1954, Corwin "Corky" Meyer took the first YF9F-9 into the air. It was powered by a Wright J65 turbojet (the American version of the British Sapphire engine) without afterburner. The first test flights showed great promise and in October of that year, the first order for forty-two aircraft was placed.

Shortly after, in April 1955, the new fighter's designation was changed to F11F-1 and it was given the name Tiger.

On March 8, 1957, the U.S. Navy began to take delivery of their new fighter. The first 42 F11F-1s were powered by the Wright J65-W-6 without afterburner. The remaining 157 aircraft were equipped with the Wright J65-W-18 with afterburner. They also incorporated a lengthened nose to accommodate an air-to-air radar that was never installed. These were known as the F11F-1 "Long Nose." Armed with four 20 mm cannon and later four Sidewinder missiles, the F11 was strictly limited to daylight operations.

A photo-reconnaissance version had been planned but was never built.

After just 201 aircraft had been delivered, the production line was shut down. A Super Tiger was produced with a more powerful engine and it was capable of Mach 2. It was 400 mph (685 km/h) faster than the F11F-1, but proved too heavy for carrier use. An attempt was made to sell the Japanese on the new fighter, but they chose the Lockheed F-104 Starfighter instead. When compared to other fighters, the F11 was an exceptional aircraft, but only six squadrons converted to Tigers (VA-156, VF-33, VF-21, VA-191, VA-121 and VF-51). Later on, two squadrons, VT-23 and VT-26, adopted the Tiger as their advanced trainer. For two years, from 1957 to 1959, the F11 Tiger served for short spells aboard the carriers USS *Ranger, Intrepid, Forrestal, Saratoga,* and *Bon Homme Richard.*

The Tiger's service was extremely short, and as soon as the F8 Crusader became available, they were quickly replaced by the more advanced fighter. The F11's short-range and persistent engine problems proved its downfall, but remarkably it was accepted by the world-famous "Blue Angels" and served with the aerobatic team until 1968.

Above: The F11 was strictly a clear-weather day fighter. Its limited range and lack of radar restricted its operational use. Right: Four F11F-1s from VF-21 in formation.

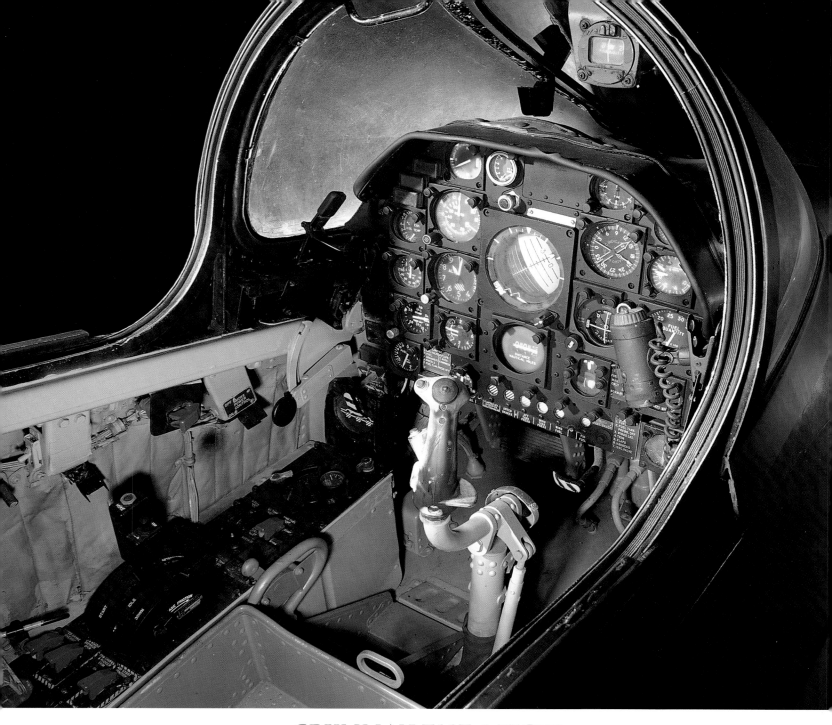

GRUMMAN F11F-1 TIGER
National Museum of Naval Aviation, Pensacola, Florida

1. Speed Brake/Nozzle Open Override Switches
2. Yaw Damper and Rudder Trim/Air Start Ignition Switches
3. Throttle with Mike Switch
4. Speed Brakes Switch
5. Smoke Power Control Switch
6. Engine Fuel/Fuel Tank Transfer Switches
7. Landing Gear Lever
8. Oxygen Regulator

9. Canopy Release Handle
10. Landing Gear Emergency Manual Release
11. Wheels and Flaps Position Indicator
12. Engine Warning Lights
13. Exhaust Temp Gauge
14. Tachometer
15. Engine Pressure Radio Indicator
16. Fuel Flow Indicator

17. Angle-of-Attack Indicator
18. Airspeed Indicator
19. Altimeter
20. Rate-of-Climb Indicator
21. Oil Pressure Indicator
22. Elevator Trim Control
23. Control Stick
24. Radar Range Meter
25. Attitude Indicator
26. Range Indicator

27. Flaps Locked Indicator
28. Speed Brakes Indicator
29. Aft Tanks Pressure Indicator
30. Wing Tank Pressure Indicator
31. Wing Fuel Indicator
32. Fin Fuel Indicator
33. Compass
34. Clock
35. Course Indicator
36. Cross Pointer Course Indicator

37. Turn-and-Bank Indicator
38. Accelerometer
39. Fuel Quantity Gauge
40. Cockpit Light
41. Flight System Hydraulic Pressure Gauge
42. Fast Gyro Erect Button
43. Bombs and Rockets Switch
44. Throttle Friction Control
45. Rudder Pedal Adjustment Handle

PILOT'S PERSPECTIVE
Rear Admiral Skip Furlong
U.S. Navy (Ret.)

I first flew the F11 in 1957. I went through flight training in about nine months, but I never carrier qualified during my training. The first time I saw a carrier was in a fully loaded F11 in the Pacific!

The F11 was not a big airplane and the cockpit was sized accordingly, although to me it was state-of-the-art. In those days we didn't have what we called RAGS, which were training squadrons for each type of aircraft in the fleet. We just sat down with the book and a mentor, read it over, and when you were ready to go you went.

The first unusual thing you realized in an F11 was to do with the field take-off. It took awhile. The J65 wasn't that powerful an engine. The F11 was a clean airplane, though, and once it got going it flew quite well. And when you kicked the burner in, that was something else. During the Formosa Crisis, it's fortunate that the airplane never went into combat. The F11 didn't have the desired range, endurance or load-carrying capacity for effective combat, although it was the best available at the time. We were the last to launch and the first to recover. That's why I have 900 sorties, but only 810 hours.

Everything in the cockpit was close to hand and somewhat familiar because I had flown previous Grumman products. It was a very comfortable cockpit and a very comfortable airplane. The quarter visibility was not that good. The F11 didn't have a true bubble canopy, so you didn't see as well as you'd like. The workload in the cockpit was not that significant, except around the boat. Around the ship, the F11 was the type of aircraft that required a great deal of attention. Usually you were fairly low on fuel. The aircraft was also underpowered in the approach configuration. Add to that the high approach-speed of the F11 on a hot Pacific day, and you could get into trouble very quickly. The fuel gauge in the F11 was also not that accurate. I ended up having to dead-stick several F11s, one into Edwards one time with 500 pounds still showing on the gauge. It was somewhat notorious.

The F11 cockpit had a good air-conditioning system. Everything by and large was in a logical position, but the F11 cockpit was small. When you got into an air-combat maneuvering situation, you'd bang you head on the canopy.

The F11 was honest as the day is long, you could fly it as fast as it would go and still feel comfortable in it.

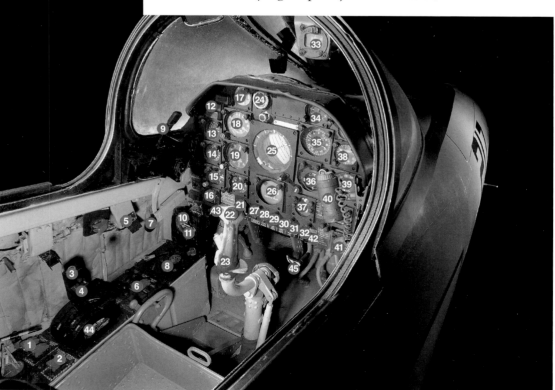

PILOT'S PERSPECTIVE
Rear Admiral Paul Gillcrist
U.S. Navy (Ret.)

The F8 was the most difficult carrier airplane to land, ever. Its approach speed was fairly rapid, but that wasn't the problem. It was the speed instability. It took an enormous amount of work to land the F8. Consider the following statistic: there were something like 1,266 F8s built and there were 1,148 major accidents in them.

When I first sat in the F8 cockpit, it was very large compared to everything else I had flown — the F11 Tiger, the F9F Panther, the Hellcat. The F8, while bigger than other aircraft I have flown, had a cockpit that was not very large, and the seat was very hard. The comfort level on long flights was not good. I recently had the opportunity to sit in an F8 cockpit while I was on location in the Philippines shooting the film *13 Days*. After all these years, I remember saying to myself, my God, this is small.

For the most part the controls and instruments were close to hand and easy to reach. It was not a badly organized cockpit. Probably the hardest thing to do in the cockpit after you made a carrier landing was get the wing-fold mechanisms started. It was something you had to practice. It was vital to get the wings up quickly and the aircraft across the foul line and cleared for the next airplane. It was a multi-step mechanism that you operated with your right hand. While you were doing that, you were also taxiing the airplane with your left hand on the control stick and your feet on the rudder pedals. It was a busy minute or two after you landed.

The rearward visibility in the F8 was awful. For a fighter, you want good rearward visibility, and the F8 simply didn't have it. As a matter of fact, it was not a lot worse than the Phantom. The F8 was single-seater, and so we had to operate the radar as well. We got pretty good at it. In the cockpit you had a handle that enabled you to steer it. With your right hand on the stick and your left on the radar handle, you could point the radar antenna and do a number of things with it — lock on and spot lighting, and so on. I had the pleasure of flying the F8 Crusader for twelve years and it was probably the longest-legged high-performance fighter ever made.

VOUGHT F8A CRUSADER
National Museum of Naval Aviation, Pensacola, Florida

1. Wing Incidence Handle
2. Fire Control Panel
3. Fuel Control Switch
4. Radar Control Panel
5. Rudder Trim Control
6. Emergency Brake Handle
7. Throttle
8. Landing Gear Handle
9. Emergency Downlock Release Switch
10. Inflight Refueling Probe Light
11. Landing Gear Position Indicators
12. Inflight Refueling Probe Switch
13. Tachometer
14. Engine Pressure Radio Indicator
15. Exhaust Temp Indicator
16. Engine Oil Pressure Indicator
17. Angle-of-Attack Indicator
18. Turn-and-Bank Indicator
19. Acceleration Indicator
20. Fire Warning Light
21. Radio Altitude Indicator
22. Airspeed Machmeter
23. Altimeter
24. AN/APS-67 Radar Scope
25. Attitude Indicator
26. Elevon Trim Control
27. Control Stick
28. Engine Fuel Pump Warning Light
29. Course Indicator
30. Radio Magnetic Indicator
31. Rocket Pack Fire Light
32. Fuel Quantity Test Switch
33. Armament Panel
34. Compass
35. Fuel Dump Switch
36. Clock
37. Fuel Flow Indicator
38. Rate-of-Climb Indicator
39. Standby Attitude Indicator
40. Fuel Transfer Switch
41. UHF Channel Preset Indicator
42. Transfer Fuel Quantity Indicator
43. Fuel Quantity Gauge
44. Ejection Seat Handle

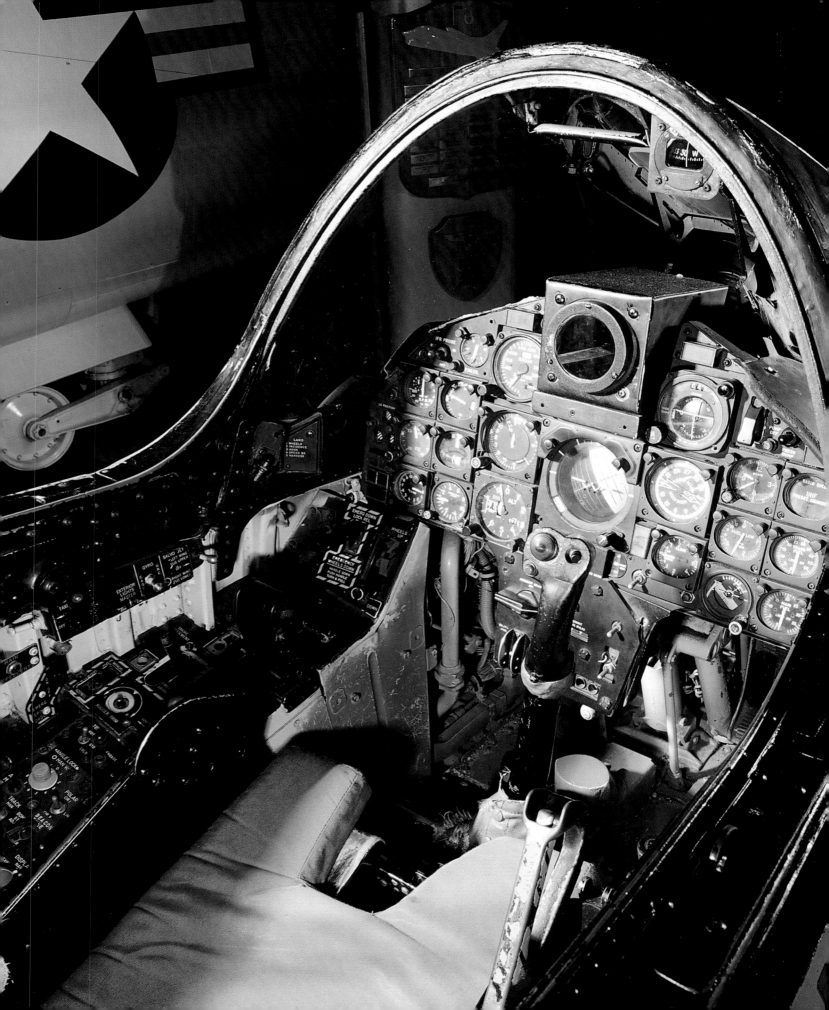

GLOSTER METEOR

HAWKER HUNTER

GLOSTER JAVELIN

ENGLISH ELECTRIC
LIGHTNING

HAWKER
SEA HAWK

SUPERMARINE
SCIMITAR

UNITED KINGDOM

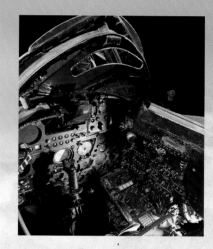

**DE HAVILLAND
SEA VIXEN**

AVRO VULCAN

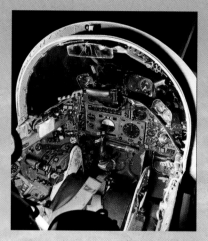

**BLACKBURN
BUCCANEER**

**ENGLISH ELECTRIC
CANBERRA**

VICKERS VALIANT

HANDLEY PAGE VICTOR

GLOSTER
METEOR

OBSOLETE WHEN IT FIRST ENTERED SERVICE, THE GLOSTER METEOR F.8 MADE UP THE BULK OF RAF FIGHTER COMMAND FROM 1950 TO 1956 AND PROVED TO BE AN EFFECTIVE FIRST-GENERATION COLD WAR FIGHTER.

On March 5, 1943, Britain's first jet fighter took to the air. Although underpowered and lacking maneuverability at high altitude, the Meteor Mk I was still faster than any of its piston-engined stablemates, especially at low and medium altitudes. Originally designed as a high-altitude interceptor, the Meteor was rushed into action to counter the world's first cruise missile, Germany's V-1. The Meteor first entered service with 616 Squadron in July 1944. Armed with four 20 mm Hispano cannons, the new jets soon began to take their share of V-1s. In early 1945, the faster and more maneuverable Mk III entered service and 616 Squadron moved to Belgium and then the Netherlands. Their mission was high-altitude interception of German Me 262s and Arado 234 jet bombers, but they never intercepted these formidable aircraft. The Meteor was finally used in the ground-attack role.

By 1947, the Meteor had been in production for just over four years, and the Mk 4 was in front-line service. The rapid development of jet-fighter design and engine thrust meant a major design change was needed to improve the Meteor's performance. The new Meteor was designated the F.8 and would be Britain's number-one fighter from 1950 until 1955. It would also be the only British jet fighter to see extensive combat service after the end of the Second World War, but not with the RAF.

The new F.8 was longer, by 30 inches (76 cm), had more powerful engines — two Rolls-Royce Derwent 8s, each developing 3,500 pounds (1,590 kg) of thrust — and had a new vertical tailplane. The new fighter was a great improvement and general handling was described as being easy and delightful at all speeds. The first F.8 was delivered to the RAF's 43 Squadron on August 2, 1949.

Ironically, during the Korean War, both the RAF and Fleet Air Arm did not send jet fighters to the theater. It was up to the Royal Australian Air Force (RAAF) to show what the Meteor could do. In 1951, 77 Squadron of the RAAF, which had been flying North American F-15 Mustangs, began to re-equip with the new F.8 Meteor. The disadvantages of the F.8 were quickly apparent. The swept-wing MiG-15 was extremely efficient at high altitude, while the Meteor was slower and less maneuverable at height.

On July 22, 1951, 77 Squadron flew its first Meteor mission in concert with a group of F-86 Sabres, but it was not until August 29 did the Meteors see action. In a fighter sweep over Chongju, eight F.8s flew into "MiG Alley" and tangled with about thirty MiG-15s. One aircraft was lost with the pilot taken prisoner. It was clearly evident that the Meteor was no match for the MiG-15. By the end of 1951, the Meteor had been pressed into the ground-attack role and there it served with great distinction. Its rugged construction and low-altitude performance were perfect for the role. At the end of the Korean War in July 1953, 77 Squadron RAAF racked up an impressive 18,872 sorties for a loss of forty-two pilots, thirty-two in Meteors. To their credit, they managed to shoot down three MiG-15s.

A total of 1,183 F.8s were built and served with the RAF, RAAF, the Danish, Dutch, Belgium, Egyptian, Syrian, Brazilian and Israeli air forces.

Today a number of restored Meteors still fly in private hands, and one is still hard at work with the Martin Baker Company testing ejection seats.

Left: A Meteor T.7 in a vertical dive. The T.7 first entered service in December 1948 and was the RAF's first jet trainer. Above: A Meteor F.8 of 77 Squadron RAAF at K-14 Kimpo Air Base near Seoul, Korea.

PILOT'S PERSPECTIVE
Air Vice-Marshal Ron Dick
RAF (Ret.)

To young lads newly graduated from flying training on Harvards (T.6s), the cockpit of a first-generation jet such as the Meteor came as something of a shock. The altimeter had more needles, the airspeed was in knots instead of mph, and the engine instruments looked odd. There were air brakes, fuel cock levers and relight buttons. Just starting the Rolls-Royce Derwents could be alarming. When an engine start button was pressed, a low moaning began. Five seconds or so later, the undercarriage lights dimmed, and the appropriate high-pressure cock was moved to the half-open position. As engine rpm rose, the HP cock was eased slowly to the fully open position. Hasty moves induced a resonance that shook the whole aircraft.

The most significant difference between the piston engine and early jets was throttle response. Rapid movement of the throttle in either direction could lead to a flame-out, and engines were not enthusiastic about starting above 15,000 feet. The capacity of the batteries was limited, so it was important to make the first start count. However, the designers of the early Meteors had forgotten that, during a relight attempt, a pilot needed to continue flying the aircraft. The high-pressure cocks were low down on either side of the seat, and the relight buttons (which had to be kept pressed while the engine was winding up) were on the instrument panel. The pilot had to grip the stick with his knees, press the relight button for five seconds, then open the HP cock slowly while keeping the button pressed, and wait to see if the engine responded. A double engine flame-out offered a particular challenge, especially below 5,000 feet. The early Martin Baker ejection seat was "manual," and the pilot had to separate himself from the seat once clear of the aircraft.

These things in mind, the Meteor was a pleasure to fly. The view from inside the clear bubble canopy was a revelation. However, it was necessary to temper euphoria with caution. There was then virtually no internal radar coverage over Britain and the Meteor cockpit had no navigational equipment to speak of. When the fuel gauges showed full, a Meteor had 595 gallons, enough for an average sortie length of an hour or a little less.

GLOSTER METEOR F MK 8
Imperial War Museum, Duxford, England

1. Pneumatic Triple Pressure Gauge
2. VHF Sets Changeover Switch
3. UHF Transmit Tone Switch
4. Throttle
5. UHF Emergency Transmit Switch
6. Port Engine Fire Warning Light and Indicator Light Switch
7. Telebriefing Press-to-Speak Button and Warning Light
8. Flap Lever
9. Airbrakes Control
10. Engine Starting Pushbuttons
11. LP Pumps Circuit Breakers
12. Battery Isolating Switch
13. Bomb/Wing Drop Tanks Jettison Control
14. Flap Position Indicator
15. Landing Lamp Switch
16. Undercarriage Lever
17. Undercarriage Position Indicator
18. Machmeter
19. Airspeed Indicator
20. Altimeter
21. Gun Button
22. Rocket and Bombs Safety Catch
23. Oil Pressure Gauge
24. Control Stick
25. Standby Compass
26. Artificial Horizon
27. Gyro Compass
28. Fuel Quantity Gauges
29. Generator Failure Warning Lights
30. CGS Circuit Breaker
31. Rate-of-Climb Indicator
32. Turn-and-Slip Indicator
33. Instrument Panel Lamps Dimmer
34. Oil Pressure Gauge
35. Fire Engine Warning Light
36. Tachometer
37. Exhaust Gas Temp Gauge
38. Hydraulic Hand Pump

HUNTER

REGARDED BY MANY AS THE BEST-LOOKING AND BEST-HANDLING COMBAT FIGHTER
OF THE 1950s, THE HAWKER HUNTER, FOR ALL ITS OUTSTANDING QUALITIES, SAW LESS
AIR COMBAT THAN THE F-86 AND MiG-15 AND WAS PRODUCED IN FEWER NUMBERS!

The Hawker Hunter was the last in a long line of outstanding fighters designed by Sydney Camm. The genius of his design began with the Hawker Fury, the most successful biplane fighter of the thirties. World War II saw the contributions made by the incomparable Hawker Hurricane, Typhoon and Tempest. This was followed by the Sea Fury, one of the fastest prop-driven aircraft ever, and his first jet fighter, the Hawker Sea Hawk.

The first Hunter prototype (P.1067) was completed in June 1951 and flew for the first time on July 20, with Hawker's chief test pilot, Squadron Leader Neville F. Duke, at the controls. Early flights were remarkably trouble free, and within months speeds had reached 700 mph (1,125 km/h). But the new fighter was not ready for squadron service. The Hunter would suffer through a prolonged gestation period. The Hunter's faults were so numerous the first twenty-one production F.1s and seven F.2s were all needed for flight testing. The first big snag was the lack of an air brake. Side-mounted air brakes that worked well on the F-86 and MiG-15 caused excessive pitch problems on the Hunter. It was finally decided to mount the air brake on the Hunter's belly, although this ruled out its use in landing. Another major problem was with the Hunter's four 30 mm cannon armament. When the guns were fired at altitude, the Avon engine surged. The powerful cannons also fatigued the surrounding structure. One by one these problems were solved, and in 1952, after evaluation by the Central Fighter Establishment, the Aeroplane and Armament Experimental Establishment and tested and approved by the USAF, U.S. funding was provided for 958 Hunters.

In July 1954, 43 Squadron became the first RAF unit to be equipped with Hunter F.1s, followed by 257 Squadron with F.2s. Early versions of the Hunter also suffered from not having a "flying tail" like the F-86. Elevator effectiveness at high Mach numbers reduced maneuverability, but unfortunately, production overtook development and it was not until the F.6 entered service that the Hunter had a fully powered elevator. The F.6 entered service with 19 Squadron in May 1956 and would eventually equip nineteen front-line squadrons. In total, 383 F.6s were built. Powered by the Avon 203 engine, the F.6 version of the Hunter was arguably the best sub-sonic fighter ever produced. Eager to update their armed forces to the same standard as the RAF, European nations quickly chose the Hunter as their fighter of choice. In all, 376 Hunters were used by the Dutch, Swiss, and Belgium air forces. Other nations wanted the Hunter as well, and many received converted and refurbished versions, including Jordan, Peru, India, Kuwait, Iraq, Saudi Arabia, Chile, Lebanon, Qatar, Kenya, Singapore and Abu Dhabi. Of the 1,972 new-build Hunters, 595 were eventually refurbished and upgraded for export, the majority of them the FGA.9 ground-attack version.

By 1958, the Hunter was purely a ground-attack fighter and it served with RAF Strike Command for almost nine years after. Today, Sydney Camm's famous fighter continues to fly. Zimbabwe still has ten Hunter FGA.9s on strength, and the Target Tug Flight of the Indian Air Force at Kalaikunda continues to use the remarkable Hawker Hunter.

Left: Five Hunter F.6s of the famous Black Arrows flying line abreast. Several aerobatic teams were formed by RAF Hunter units, but none were as famous as 111 Squadron's Black Arrows. Above: A Hunter F.6 in the standard gray-green camouflage color scheme of the day. Like the F-86, the Hunter was a true "pilot's aeroplane" with flawless handling and few limitations.

PILOT'S PERSPECTIVE
Air Chief Marshal Sir Patrick Hine
RAF (Ret.)

I first flew the Hunter F.6 on May 23, 1957 upon joining 111(F) Squadron, famous for their "Black Arrows" formation aerobatic team of 1957–60. I logged over 1,200 flying hours in the F.6. It was very much a pilot's aircraft — probably my favorite — and a delight to fly.

Access to the pressurized cockpit was via a special-to-type ladder, but there was a single emergency foot-step on the port side of the forward fuselage. The pilot sat in a Martin Baker Mk 2H (later 3H with a 100-feet capability in level flight). The seat could become somewhat hard on longer sorties. Forward and side-ways visibility from the cockpit was excellent but there was a blind spot when looking rearward below the tailplane.

When I first sat in the Hunter, I knew instinctively that I was about to fly a thoroughbred. The cockpit was typically British: narrower and less spacious than those of contemporary American fighters, but nonetheless large and comfortable enough. It had a conventional layout consisting of a front facia with side panels under the coaming (the flight instruments panel being central at eye level) and two flat consoles either side of the pilot. All of the essential controls and switches could be operated, with the exception of the radios and IFF, with the pilot hardly having to move his head, but some test switches, circuit breakers and accumulator-pressure gauges at the rear of the side consoles were difficult to handle or read in flight.

The RT transmit button and air-brake-control switch were conveniently positioned on the throttle, while the elevator-trim switch, armament safety flap, trigger and cine-camera button were all on the top of the control column (the "stick") which was molded to fit the pilot's right hand.

While changing radio frequencies in cloud or formation was slightly tricky, requiring a quick look down to check the new setting, the radio knobs were very close to the throttle and thus quite easy to locate with the left hand. My own minor criticisms of the cockpit layout were that the hydraulic and generator-failure warning lights were partially hidden under the left coaming and behind the "stick," respectively, while the aileron spring-feel trim attached to the lower part of the control column had to be operated with the left hand, which required moving it momentarily from the throttle. Overall, the F.6's cockpit ergonomics for an aircraft of the 1950s era were excellent.

HAWKER HUNTER F.6
Imperial War Museum, Duxford, England

1. Tail Parachute Switch and Indicator
2. RP Selector Switch
3. Bomb Master Switch
4. Radar Presentation Switch
5. Target Rejection Switch
6. Fuel Flow Level Warning Lights
7. Clear Aircraft Push Switch
8. Accelerometer
9. Elevator Power Control Switch
10. Aileron Power Control Indicator
11. Emergency Flap Control
12. Triple Pressure Gauge
13. Gyro Gunsight Control Unit
14. Bomb Fusing Switch
15. RP Ripple Switch
16. Tail Plane Position Indicator
17. Machmeter
18. Flap Control
19. Hood Jettison Control
20. Standby Compass
21. Gyro Gunsight
22. Airspeed Indicator
23. Altimeter
24. Flap Position Indicator
25. Camera Gun Push Switch
26. Gun Button Safety Covers
27. Tail Plane Incidence Control Switch
28. Control Stick
29. Bombs RP Selector Switch
30. Artificial Horizon
31. Gyro Compass
32. Oil Pressure Gauge
33. Ignition Switch
34. Starter Push Switch
35. Engine Master Switches
36. Standby Altimeter
37. Rate-of-Climb Indicator
38. Turn-and-Slip Indicator
39. Turn-and-Slip Supply Emergency Switch
40. Generator Warning Lights
41. Fire Warning Light and Extinguisher
42. Tachometer
43. Clock
44. Gyro Gunsight Master Switch

GLOSTER

JAVELIN

As the world's first operational delta-winged fighter, the Gloster Javelin would prove to be one of the RAF's most effective all-weather interceptors with a performance comparable to the superb single-seat Hawker Hunter.

The origin of the Javelin began with two project studies prepared to meet British Air Staff requirements calling for a day interceptor and a day and night interceptor. The design team at Gloster proposed a delta-wing design to meet the new stipulations. Enthusiasm for the delta-wing platform sprang from the availability of German wartime research conducted by Dr. Alexander Lippisch and in February 1948, RAF night-fighter needs crystallized in the form of specification F.4/4.8.

When the prototype first appeared as G.A.5, the new Gloster fighter was described as the RAF's first purpose-designed all-weather jet interceptor and the heaviest to enter service. The G.A.5 was a big aircraft and was easily recognized by its massive, highly swept fin and fixed-delta tailplane. At the time the new G.A.5 was an impressive-looking machine and, for a fighter, as compared to the Gloster Meteor or de Havilland Vampire, quite massive. Overall length and wingspan were over 50 feet (15 m) and the fin towered 16 feet (5 m) above the ground. Powered by two Sapphire turbojets each offering 7,000 pounds (3,180 kg) thrust, the first prototype flew on November 26, 1951. In July 1952, the RAF ordered the G.A.5 into super-priority production as the Javelin.

But all was not well with the RAF's new all-weather fighter. On June 29, G.A.5 was destroyed after it suddenly developed elevator flutter while investigating high-speed handling at low level. Test pilot Bill Waterton managed to reach the threshold of the runway at Boscombe Down before losing control and crashing into the ground heavily. The aircraft caught fire, but Bill Waterton managed to escape with all the vital flight data intact and was awarded the George Medal for his efforts. The gestation period for the Javelin proved to be a long and protracted affair. It was not until the fifth prototype flew in July 1954 that the first production Javelin FAW.1 left the line two days later. This was followed by an order worth 36.8 million British pounds placed by the USAF on behalf of its off-shore Mutual Defense Aid Program.

The first unit to receive the new all-weather fighter was 46 Squadron in February 1956. Tasked with the job of evaluating the Javelin in squadron strength, the pilots of 46 Squadron soon showed their new mount was a formidable all-weather fighter, well equipped to counter Soviet manned bombers coming over the North Sea. Armed with four 30 mm cannons, the Javelin could reach 50,000 feet in under ten minutes and was just as fast as the single-seat Hawker Hunter. The introduction of the FAW.7 version of the Javelin in 1956 ushered in the air-to-air missile age. The FAW.7's primary armament was four Firestreak infrared AAMs, supplement by two 30 mm cannon, and at the time it was one of most heavily armed fighters in the world. The last version to see service with the RAF was the FAW.9. These aircraft were equipped with American radar and a pair of Sapphire 7R engines, which produced more agile performance above 20,000 feet. There were 127 Javelin 7s converted to FAW.9s, and of these, 40 were given in-flight refueling capability.

In 1968, 60 Squadron was the last to fly the Javelin in front-line service. It was soon superseded by the BAC Lightning. However, a red and white Javelin FAW.9 continued flying, doing valuable flight research at Boscombe Down until January 1975. It is now part of the Imperial War Museum Collection at Duxford.

Right: The FAW.4 first appeared in September 1955. It introduced a fully powered all-moving tailplane. Fifty were built.

PILOT'S PERSPECTIVE
Brian Carroll
RAF (Ret.)

The Javelin cockpit was something of a surprise, coming from an instructor's tour on Vampires. It was cavernous by comparison — unusually so for a British fighter, as most fighter cockpits were, if nothing else, economic on space. The nav/rads rear cockpit was even larger. With the seat fully lowered, he disappeared from sight.

The cockpit layout was pretty conventional for its day. I flew the Mk 5s; Mk 9s and the Mk 9R (the flight-refueling version) and, of course, the trainer version, the T.3. The main flight instruments were centered. They were, however, slightly obscured by the control column, which meant one had to peer around it on occasions in order to check the RPM gauges, which were sited low, down below the main panel.

Since the Javelin was an all-weather fighter, cockpit lighting was very good, though it was always kept at a minimal level to allow the pilot to retain good night vision. The large canopy provided excellent all-round vision, especially important in combat. The nav/rad in the rear seat was particularly valuable in keeping a lookout in the six o'clock position, making it difficult for the opposition to sneak in astern.

The T.3's emergency undercarriage lowering was difficult to operate. I experienced this on my first solo when the port main leg remained locked fully up. All efforts at recycling and pulling G proved fruitless. The control to activate the emergency lowering was positioned well behind the front seat. One had to reach back with the left arm, rotate it clockwise virtually at full length to pull the cable, with the arm in such a position it lacked any degree of strength and was quite hard to pull. Needless to say I managed, and the reluctant port leg finally locked down, giving me three greens for an uneventful landing.

The Javelin's cockpit was spacious and comfortable. Instrumentation was such that one was confident in the worst of conditions, even operating at night, at low level, on occasions to 250 feet AMSL and 500 feet AGL.

Nicknamed the "Dragmaster" and "Flat Iron," the large delta-wing Javelin garnered its share of bad press, but was admired by the many pilots who flew it.

GLOSTER JAVELIN FAW.9
Imperial War Museum, Duxford, England

1. VHF Emergency Switches
2. Static Cable Cutter Switches
3. Ventral Tanks Jettison Handle
4. Throttle Quadrant
5. Reheat Master Switches
6. Cockpit Light
7. Rudder Pedals
8. Hood Jettison Handle
9. Cockpit Light
10. Accelerometer
11. ILS Marker and Zero Reader
12. Zero Reader Control Unit
13. Hood Jettison Handle Safety Pin and Flag
14. Radio Altimeter
15. ILS Indicator
16. Fuel Quantity Gauge
17. Control Stick

18. Standby Accelerometer
19. Airspeed Indicator
20. Radio Altimeter Height Band Selector
21. Anti-Dazzle Switch
22. Gun Trigger Safety Catch
23. Camera Button
24. Fuel Transfer Air Pressure Warning Light
25. Ejection Seat Handle
26. Tailplane Trimmer Switch
27. Gyro Compass
28. Machmeter
29. Rate-of-Climb Indicator
30. Turn-and-Slip Indicator
31. Port Engine Fire Extinguisher
32. Tachometers
33. Dual Jet Pipe Temp Gauge
34. Jet Pipe Nozzle Indicators

35. Oxygen Contents Gauge
36. Compass Gyro Selector Switch
37. Booster Pump Warning Lights
38. Windscreen Rain Dispersal Control
39. Cockpit Altimeter
40. Oil Pressure Gauge
41. Parking Brake Control
42. Oxygen Regulator
43. Switch Row - De-misting, Anti-Icing
44. Cockpit Lighting Dimmer Controls
45. Hydraulic Pump Failure Warning Lights
46. Hydraulic Pressure Gauges
47. Low Speed/Stall Warning On/Off Switch
48. Emergency Oxygen Control
49. ILS Control Unit

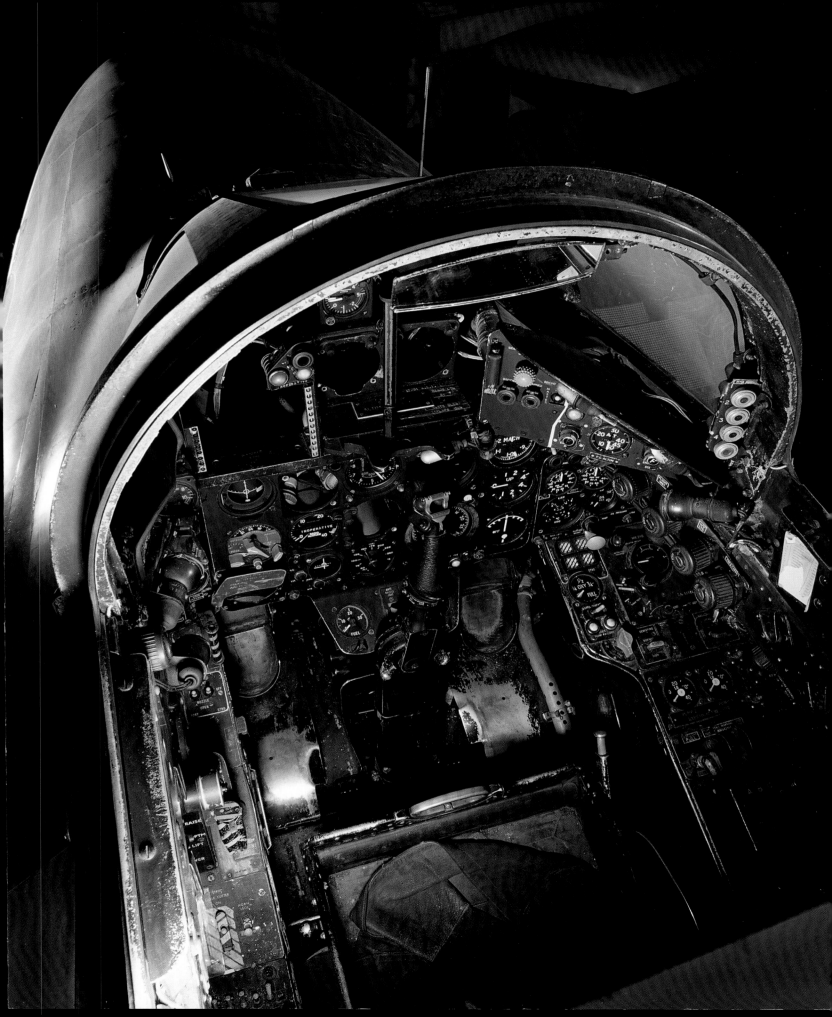

ENGLISH ELECTRIC

LIGHTNING

Its angular shape and over-under engine arrangement gave the Lightning the appearance of barely controlled speed. Britain's first supersonic fighter proved to be the best point-defense fighter of the Cold War.

In 1947, Britain's major fighter manufacturers were all still busy developing and building conventional subsonic aircraft. Hawker Aircraft was building piston-engine Sea Furies and developing the straight-wing, jet-engine Sea Hawk. Supermarine built Spitfires until October 1947 and had flown only two prototypes of the jet-engine naval fighter, the Attacker. Meanwhile, in that same month the Americans had flown the prototype for the swept-wing F-86 Sabre! America was beginning to take the lead in fighter design, but the Second World War had brought a number of newcomers into the fighter business. One of these was English Electric, which re-entered the aviation business just in time for the pre-war buildup and spent the war as a straight aircraft manufacturer.

In 1947, English Electric won a contract to study the design of an M-1.5 experimental research aircraft. This was later revised to include guns and a sighting system to see if supersonic fighters would prove practical. The Project 1 or P.1 design featured wings swept sharply back at 60 degrees and two engines arranged one above the other and fed from a simple nose air intake. The P.1 made its first flight on August 4, 1954, and went supersonic on its third flight. The next step was the P.1B, which would form the basis for an operational fighter. This aircraft was fitted with radar, two 30 mm cannons and two de Havilland Blue Jay (Firestreak) infrared homing missiles on fuselage pylons. It also received more powerful engines and a raised canopy to improve the view to the rear. The P.1B was the first example of a weapon systems concept produced by the British aircraft industry. Twenty pre-series aircraft were ordered. In 1958, the new fighter was named Lightning. By the end of June 1960, the RAF had taken delivery of the first Lightning F.1s.

The following year, 74 Squadron was declared operational with the first and last British-designed supersonic fighter. Better versions were to follow: the F.1A with in flight air-to-air re-fueling capability; the F.2 — although almost identical to the F.1A, it had engines with much-needed fully variable reheat; and the F.3, probably the hottest of the entire series with more reliable and powerful engines and an improved fire-control system armed with two Red Top collision-course IR missiles. The F.3 was also fitted with a larger fin to help cope with directional stability at higher speeds. The last version to enter RAF service was the F.6 and was, in essence, a late-model F.3 with all the long-range modifications incorporated into it. The F.6 gained weight with the addition of a massive 600-gallon (2,730 L) fuel tank, which created less drag than the original 250-gallon (1,125 L) tank.

RAF Lightning strength reached a peak in 1968–70 with nine front-line squadrons operational. Export versions were also sold to Saudi Arabia and Kuwait. Phasing out of the Lightning began in 1971. The Lightning's replacement would be the McDonnell Douglas F-4 Phantom, followed by the Air Defense Version of the Tornado. Delay of the Tornado ADV forced the RAF to maintain two Lightning squadrons until 1988, when they were finally retired from service.

When the Lightning first entered service with the RAF, it was the world's only pure supersonic fighter and would stay that way until the advent of the McDonnell Douglas F-15. What the Lightning lacked in endurance and armament, it more than made up for it in raw performance. For many years the Lightning was the world's finest supersonic point-defense fighter, and in terms of top speed, rate of climb and service ceiling, it is still better than the Panavia Tornado built to replace it.

Right: Lightnings of 74 Squadron peel off for the camera.
These Lightning F.6s are armed with the heat-seeking Firestreak missile.

PILOT'S PERSPECTIVE
Brian Carroll
RAF (Ret.)

My first experience of flying the Lightning was in July of 1965, in XS419, the side-by-side two-seat trainer. After a tour on Javelins, the cockpit was by comparison somewhat cramped, especially when both pilots were in full flying kit. I had just qualified as a Lightning flight simulator instructor, so it was going to be a while before I flew the Lightning on a regular basis. However, the simulator was a single-seat version, so it gave me ample opportunity to evaluate the ergonomics of the cockpit.

It was certainly less spacious than the Javelin, but more than adequate. "Snug" might well be the right word. All controls fell easily to hand and the instrument presentation was excellent. The main flight display (OR 946) comprised a combined strip speed and mach display, and below this was the attitude indicator, which also incorporated a "flight director bead" coupled to the auto-pilot. The center of the compass provided space for either the TACAN and or the ILS. If desired, the TACAN could be displayed while flying an ILS approach using the flight director bead. The main altimeter and RCDI were fairly standard.

The remaining instrumentation was sensibly distributed around the cockpit; control for the radar sited by the throttles was comfortable and easy to use; trim switches and auto-pilot engage switches were on the control column; warning lights indicating any emergencies were easily seen. The cockpit, though "snug," was comfortable, even after an extended trip. With flight refueling, eight-hour trips were not unknown.

I flew all marks of the Lightning, and although there were differences — the early marks had more conventional instrumentation — the general layout was always more than acceptable.

The Lightning was easy and very pleasant to fly, but not so simple to operate as a weapons system. The radar display was situated on the left side of the cockpit, and while the pilot was assessing targets, the auto-pilot came into its own, using "attitude hold" to ensure that the aircraft maintained the desired flight path while the pilot briefly peered into the scope.

Visibility was restricted to the rear; it was possible to check one's "six" but not easily. Forward and side to side visibility was excellent.

Overall, the cockpit was user friendly, a nice layout, and the controls conveniently sited.

ENGLISH ELECTRIC LIGHTNING F.6
Lightning Preservation Group,
Bruntingthorpe, England

1. Engine Relight Buttons
2. Cockpit Light
3. Fire Extinguisher Switch/Indicators
4. AI Radar Handle Controller
5. No 1. Engine Throttle Control
6. No. 2 Engine Throttle Control
7. Rudder Trim Switches
8. De-Ice/Rain Dispersal Switch
9. De-Ice/Rain Dispersal Indicator
10. Feel Switch
11. Undercarriage Selector
12. Standard Warning Panel
13. Spare Bulbs
14. Services Hydraulic System Pressure Gauge
15. Stores Jettison Button

16. Standby Direction Indicator
17. Flight Refueling Panel
18. Instrument Power Supply Indicator
19. Normal/Standby Inverter Switch
20. Brake Parachute Jettison Switch
21. Standby Airspeed Indicator
22. Hook Down Indicator Light
23. Alternator and Generator Field Reset Buttons
24. Audio Alarm Mute Switch
25. Arrester Hook Handle
26. Brake Parachute Steam Handle
27. Brake Accumulator Pressure Gauge
28. Standby Altimeter
29. Main Altimeter

30. Flaps Position Indicator
31. Standby Artificial Horizon
32. Trigger Guard
33. Attitude Indicator
34. Navigation Display
35. FCS Engage Switch
36. Aileron and Tailplane Trim Switches
37. Camera Switch
38. Light Fighter Sight Caging Switch
39. Control Column
40. Undercarriage Position Indicator
41. Combined Trim and Airbrake Position Indicator
42. Auto-pilot Trim Indicator
43. MRG Fast Erection Switch
44. MRG On/Off Switch
45. U/UHF Control Unit
46. ILS Channel Selector
47. Radar Scope

HAWKER

SEA HAWK

A DELIGHT TO FLY AND A PLEASURE TO MAINTAIN, THE HAWKER SEA HAWK PROVED TO BE
ONE OF THE MOST SUCCESSFUL AND POPULAR FIGHTERS TO SEE SERVICE WITH THE ROYAL NAVY.

In the closing months of the Second World War, the reliability and power of the new turbojet engines had reached a stage where serious development of a dependable jet fighter was a real possibility. Hawker, famous for the Fury, Hurricane, Typhoon, Tempest and Sea Fury, turned its attention to the new frontier of jet fighter production and design. Early work resulted in the P.1040 single-engine jet fighter with a bifurcated jet pipe. This meant the tailpipe divided into two, instead of extending straight aft in a single cylinder from the exhaust nozzle of the engine. This innovative design gave the Sea Hawk more thrust when compared to fighters with long tailpipes. The Air Staff and the Ministry of Aircraft Production were reluctant to accept Camm's innovative bifurcated jet pipe. But as large orders for the Tempest and Fury were canceled, Hawker quickly moved forward with the P.1040 as a private venture. The predicted top speed of the P.1040 was 600 mph (965 km/h), not much faster than the Gloster Meteor then in service. The RAF quickly lost interest, but the Royal Navy was keen to see what the new fighter could do for them.

The Royal Navy saw the P.1040 as a fleet-support fighter, and in January 1946, Hawker presented the Sea Hawk as a carrier-based interceptor with an arrestor hook and folding wings. The navy accepted the new fighter, and Hawker was instructed to proceed with the production of three prototypes, powered by the 4,500-pound-thrust (2,045 kg) Nene I engine. On September 3, 1948, the first naval prototype of the Sea Hawk took to the air. This prototype was complete with folding wings, full armament (four 20 mm Hispano cannons), catapult spools and an arrester hook. In April 1949, the real tests began with deck landings and take-offs aboard the carrier HMS *Illustrious*. On November 22, Hawker received an order for 151 Sea Hawk F Mk Is, powered by the Rolls-Royce Nene engine with 5,000 pounds (2,270 kg) of thrust.

In 1951, the British government realized that bureaucratic red tape was seriously delaying the introduction of new aircraft into RAF service. The Super-Priority Program was introduced, allowing a small group of military aircraft types to have priority status in terms of materials, facilities and manpower. Two of the aircraft listed were the Hawker Sea Hawk and Hunter, but Hawker's facilities were clearly inadequate to meet both programs. Sea Hawk development and production was quickly transferred to the Armstrong Whitworth Aircraft factory in Coventry. As Armstrong Whitworth's production began to flow, deliveries of Hawker-built fighters reached the Fleet Air Arm (FAA) on March 2, 1953.

In 1956, Britain and France planned a military operation, code named Operation Musketeer, to recover control of the Suez Canal. Beyond the range of RAF fighters, the Royal Navy was given the job of providing fighter cover. Three carriers, each with two FAA Sea Hawk squadrons, took part. On the morning of October 31, the Sea Hawks squadrons from HMS *Bulwark* struck Cairo West airfield with cannons and bombs. In the first five days of the operations, FAA aircraft flew 1,300 offensive operations and had two Sea Hawks lost to ground fire.

The Dutch, German and Indian navies also ordered the Sea Hawk. In all, 542 were produced. The last unit to fly the elegant fighter was the Fleet Requirements Unit. Between 1956 and 1969, the FRU operated Sea Hawk F.1s, FB.5s and FGA.6s.

Right: A graceful shot of seven Sea Hawk FGA.6s of 800 Squadron. Because of its good power-to-weight ratio, the Sea Hawk was a superb formation aerobatic platform.

PILOT'S PERSPECTIVE
Lieutenant Commander
Peter Sheppard
AFC RN (Ret.)

I first flew the Sea Hawk in early 1954, but spent most of the previous year flying Sea Furies with 807 Squadron during the Korean War. When we came back to England, our Sea Furies were replaced with the Sea Hawk.

The Sea Hawk was such an easy airplane to fly and beautifully responsive. In fact, we formed an aerobatic team within three weeks of getting the airplane. It was very comfortable with a wonderful view. There was a great similarity between the Sea Hawk and Sea Fury cockpit layout; you could recognize that it was a Hawker aircraft. The great thing with the Sea Hawk was being able to see the ground from the cockpit. You couldn't in the Sea Fury because of the big piston engine in front of you.

The noise level in the cockpit was reduced considerably because the engine sat behind you. There was just a nice whine. In a piston-engine fighter, you basically flew it by the seat of your pants. If there was anything wrong with the engine, you felt it before the instruments would register the problem. In the Sea Hawk, you relied on your instruments rather than feel to indicate if there was anything wrong. The biggest danger was engine failure, but the Sea Hawk turned out to be one of the finest gliders in the world. It was like a little dart!

The cockpit was very comfortable. With one elbow resting on your right knee, you could have fingertip control on the stick. The left hand dropped naturally onto the rudder and aileron control trim controls. Everything was very, very natural. Being a reasonably tall chap, I always seemed to have my cockpit seat as low as I could stand. I used to find myself leaning forward in the straps to read the compass, which was in the six o'clock position on the bottom of the instrument panel. Apart from that, it was very comfortable. The other reason I had the straps fairly loose was so that I could lean forward and look over my shoulder. With the bubble canopy, you had 360-degree vision, which made deck landings a heck of a lot easier as compared to the piston-engine Sea Fury.

HAWKER SEA HAWK FGA.6
Fleet Air Arm Museum, Yeovilton, England

1. H.P. Cock Lever and Relight Button
2. Rudder/Aileron Trim Control
3. Elevator Trim Control
4. Throttle
5. Rudder/Aileron Trim Indicator
6. Airbrakes Control
7. Flaps Control
8. Undercarriage Position Indicator
9. Air Temp Gauge
10. Arrester Hook Emergency Control
11. Undercarriage Emergency Control
12. Flaps Emergency Control
13. Bomb Distributor Switch
14. Bomb Jettison Buttons
15. Hood Jettison Control
16. Arrester Hook Green Light
17. Undercarriage Selector Buttons
18. Flaps Position Indicator
19. GGS Selector/Dimmer Control
20. Anti-G Control Panel
21. Outer Bomb Selector Switches
22. Inner Bomb Selector Switches
23. Trigger Safety Covers
24. Camera Push Button
25. Control Stick
26. Gunsight
27. Fuel Tanks Fire Warning Light
28. Machmeter
29. Tachometer
30. Rudder Pedal
31. Mk. 17 Oxygen Regulator
32. Airspeed Indicator
33. Altimeter
34. Generator Failure Warning Light
35. GGS Emergency Lowering Control
36. Bottom Generator Failure Warning Light
37. Fuel Pressure Warning Light
38. Artificial Horizon
39. Gyro Compass
40. Turn-and-Slip Emergency Switch
41. Turn-and-Slip Indicator
42. Engine Fire Warning Light

SUPERMARINE
SCIMITAR

THE LAST FIGHTER DESIGNED BY SUPERMARINE WOULD PROVE A GREAT DISAPPOINTMENT. AS A HEAVY CARRIER-BORNE FIGHTER, THE SCIMITAR WAS AN UNFORGIVING FIGHTER WITH AN INCREDIBLE ACCIDENT RATE AND A REPUTATION THAT BORE NO RESEMBLANCE TO ITS FOREBEAR, THE SPITFIRE.

The Supermarine Scimitar was the Royal Navy's first swept-wing single-seat fighter and the first capable of supersonic flight in a shallow dive; it was also the last aircraft designed and built by the Supermarine division of Vickers Armstrong Aircraft.

Designed to meet Naval Spec. N113D, the Scimitar was developed through a number of prototype aircraft that included the Type 508, with a butterfly tail, and the straight-winged Type 529. Using information gained with the development of the swept-wing version of the Supermarine Attacker, Supermarine designed the swept-wing 508 and reclassified it as Type 525. Prototype 525 first flew on April 27, 1954; but on July 5, the 525 entered a spin and was destroyed. Even with this setback, an order was placed for 100 production fighters based on the 525. Improvements were needed and Supermarine developed the 525 further, producing the new 544 prototype. At the same time the single-seat fighter specification had changed. The new Scimitar would now have to serve as a low-level strike aircraft and also carry a nuclear device.

In January 1957, the first production Scimitar came off the assembly line. In order to see what the Scimitar could really do, the Navy formed a new squadron, 700X Flight. In August 1957, the unit began evaluations flights and training until May 1958. The first front-line squadron to use the type was 803, followed by 736, 800, 804, 807; 700X Flight became 700 Squadron. Scimitars operated from the carriers *Ark Royal*, *Centaur*, *Eagle* and *Hermes*, mainly in the low-level strike role. In addition to its four 30 mm Aden cannons, the Scimitar could carry a variety of stores, including four 1,000-pound (409 kg) bombs, four Bullpup air-to-surface missiles, four Sidewinder air-to-air missiles or tactical nuclear weapons.

For the Royal Navy, the Scimitar was a major leap forward, but that came at price. It constantly dripped fuel when on the ground and was described as an "unforgiving beast in the air." For the Fleet Air Arm, the problem of small carriers and large, fast aircraft meant take-offs and landings were treacherous at best. Accidents were frequent — ditchings, in-flight fires, and landing accidents. Of the 100 Scimitars ordered, only 76 were actually built (the last batch of 24 were canceled); of those, 39 were lost due to accidents and crashes for an attrition rate of over 51 percent! For all its faults, the Scimitar was a great advance in operational effectiveness for the Royal Navy. Capable of low-level nuclear strike, high-level interception with air-to-air missiles or reconnaissance at long range, the Scimitar was a very versatile and rugged aircraft. It also served in the role of aerial tanker. The early Buccaneers, which were designed to replace the Scimitar, could not take off with a full fuel load. Several Scimitars were modified with a "buddy" refueling system. This gave the Buccaneer the ability to take off with a respectable weapon load, quickly refuel with a Scimitar, and then reach its target. Although relatively short-lived in squadron service (the last front-line squadron gave up their Scimitars in October 1966), the Fleet Requirements Unit operated Scimitars, with civilian pilots, until December 1970.

Above: The last front-line role for the Scimitar began in September 1964 when 800 Squadron formed a B Flight equipped with buddy-pack refueling pods. Right: When fully loaded, the Scimitar weighed about 40,000 pounds (18,145 kg) and needed the full assistance of the steam catapult in order to take off.

PILOT'S PERSPECTIVE
Lieutenant Commander
Tom Leece
RN (Ret.)

After completing a tour duty with Sea Hawks, I joined the Scimitar X Flight at the beginning of 1954. The X Flight was comprised of many different pilots with various backgrounds. Some were test pilots, some were AWRS like me. At the time I had never flown a swept-wing fighter before. The first time I flew the Scimitar, I was given a verbal briefing, strapped in, and that was it. I then became senior pilot with 807 Squadron, and after that took command of 803 Squadron. I have about 420-odd hours in the Scimitar with a couple of night landings.

Every single chap says the same thing about the first time they flew the Scimitar, and I say it doubly so — the acceleration was incredible! Compared to the Sea Hawk cockpit, there was so much more in the Scimitar cockpit. Ergonomically speaking, it was very well laid out. Everything was easy to find. It had a 360-degree artificial horizon, whereas the Sea Hawk didn't, and you could topple it very easily in the Sea Hawk. The visibility without all the extra things such as the angle-of-attack indicators and the LAMBS equipment was quite good. But when it came to deck landing the Scimitar, the added equipment at eyeball level restricted your visibility. It was also a hell of an aircraft to fly at night. Because of the restricted cockpit visibility and the high nose-up angle required for landing, it wasn't pleasant at all.

The workload in the cockpit could be heavy at times. There was no automatic pilot in the cockpit. Some of the missions we had to do called for us to go high, steer a steady course, and then let down for a low-level run into a target you couldn't see. In those conditions, you were working like a blue-assed fly.

One of the unique things in the Scimitar cockpit was the ejection seat. It would actually work under water and the pilot could use the seat breathing apparatus to breathe while submerged.

The Scimitar was a pilot's aircraft, and it had everything you really wanted. It was a super aircraft, everything was there and I never heard anyone complain about the cockpit. But it was full. If I could have changed anything in the Scimitar cockpit, I would have made it bigger to make more room for the many instruments.

SUPERMARINE SCIMITAR F.1
Fleet Air Arm Museum, Yeovilton, England

1. Standby UHF Emergency Switches
2. IFF Fusing Inverter Switch
3. High Intensity Light Switch
4. Accelerometer
5. Port "Attention Getter" Light
6. Angle-of-Attack Indicator
7. Angle Selector Switch
8. Telebriefing Connected Light
9. Radio Altimeter Limit Lights
10. Feel Simulator Magnetic Indicator
11. LABS Switches
12. Telebriefing Call Switch
13. Blown Flaps Switch
14. Hood Clutch Lever
15. Throttle Quadrant
16. Throttles Friction Lever
17. Duplicate Trim Switch
18. Tacan Indicator
19. Barking Brake Handle
20. Arrester Hook Selector Switch
21. Flap Override Switch
22. Hood Selector Lever
23. Airbrakes Magnetic Indicator
24. Airbrakes Switch
25. Wheelbrakes Triple Pressure Gauge
26. Fuel and Engine Master Switches
27. Hood Jettison Handle
28. External Stores Jettison Switch
29. Cockpit Emergency Light Switch
30. Flaps Selector Lever
31. Radio Altimeter Height Band Selector
32. Undercarriage Position Indicator
33. Voltmeter
34. Machmeter
35. GPI Variation Setting Control
36. Tailing Edge Flaps Indicator
37. Leading Edge and Flaps Indicator
38. Tailplane Position Indicator
39. Blown Flaps On Light
40. Airspeed Indicator
41. Control Stick
42. Rudder Pedals
43. Ejection Seat Handle
44. Attitude Indicator
45. Gyro Compass
46. Hydraulic Pressure Gauges
47. JPT Control Switches
48. Rate-of-Climb Indicator
49. Artificial Horizon
50. Fuel Flowmeter
51. Flight Instrument Reset Switch
52. Inverter Fail Magnetic Indicator
53. Drop Tanks Selector Switch
54. Oxygen Flow Indicator
55. Violet Picture Indicator
56. Air-to-Air Master Refueling Switch
57. Drop Tank Fuel Transfer Indicator
58. Summation Fuel Contents Gauge
59. Valve "B" Failure Switch
60. Oil Pressure Indicators
61. Tachometer
62. JPT Indicators
63. Artificial Horizon Standby Switch
64. Fuel Contents Gauges
65. Booster Pump Warning Lights

DE HAVILLAND

SEA VIXEN

TWIN-ENGINED, TWO-PLACE, TWIN-BOOMED — THE DE HAVILLAND SEA VIXEN WAS
THE ROYAL NAVY'S FIRST ALL-WEATHER FIGHTER WITH AN ALL-MISSILE, ALL-ROCKET ARMAMENT.

Design for the Sea Vixen was initiated in 1946. The government specification called for an advanced carrier-borne all-weather fighter. The RAF issued a similar specification, and de Havilland decided that a single aircraft design could fulfill both requirements. In 1949, two prototypes of the land-based version of the fighter were ordered and designated D.H.110. The first prototype, powered by two Rolls-Royce Avon engines, flew on September 26, 1952. The second prototype flew on July 25, 1952, but crashed at Farnborough, killing the pilot, the observer and twenty-nine spectators. The flight-testing program did not resume until June 1953, and by that time the RAF had lost interest and selected the Gloster Javelin as their all-weather interceptor.

In June 1954, Navy interest returned, and the surviving prototype began a new series of trials. A navalized prototype was produced (fitted with catapult spools and arrestor hook, but lacking folding wings) and carrier trials began. The first production aircraft flew on March 20, 1957, and was fully equipped with folding wings and hinged nose radome. The first Sea Vixen was designated FAW Mk 1, and the first ten aircraft produced were allocated to 700Y Flight — the Intensive Flying Trails Unit. The first squadron, 892, was commissioned on July 2, 1959.

The Sea Vixen Mk 1's armament consisted of two retractable fuselage rocket packs housing fourteen 2-inch unguided rockets and four Firestreak infrared air-to-air missiles. Crew accommodations were similar to the Sea Venom with a side-by-side arrangement, but with the Vixen, the observer's cockpit, known as the "Coal Hole," was situated on a lower level than the pilot's. The view was almost nonexistent and was not popular with crews who flew in it.

At the time of its introduction, the Sea Vixen was a very modern fighter with a sophisticated integrated weapons system. In 1963, the improved FAW Mk 2 began to enter service. This variant had enlarged tail-booms that extended forward over the wing and allowed for more fuel and additional ECM equipment to be carried. Red Top missiles, with limited all-aspect seeker heads, replaced the tail-chase Firestreaks.

The 1960s were the Sea Vixens' most active period of service. In 1961, Iraq was threatening to invade Kuwait. The British responded by sending HMS *Victorious* to the Persian Gulf while the HMS *Bulwark* landed Royal Marines in Kuwait. Overhead Sea Vixens patrolled the skies and when a second RN carrier arrived, Iraq's President Kassem backed down. In 1964, Sea Vixens from HMS *Centaur* covered the Royal Marine landing in support of government troops in Tanganyika. In their last operation, Sea Vixens from HMS *Victorious* provided air cover with the withdrawal of British forces from Aden in 1967. The Sea Vixen was also involved with two display teams: Simon's Circus and Fred's Five.

In the early 1970s, the withdrawal of the British carrier force meant the end of the Sea Vixen. In 1972, the last Sea Vixen squadron was disbanded. Today there are several examples of the Sea Vixen in museums across England and, remarkably, there is one still flying: de Havilland Aviation Ltd., based at Hurn, maintains and flies a Sea Vixen D.3, the modified drone version.

Right: The Vixen FAW.1 was a superb air defense fighter and gave the Fleet Air Arm an aircraft with a better capability than those of most land-based air forces of the day.

PILOT'S PERSPECTIVE
Lieutenant Commander
Peter Sheppard
AFC RN (Ret.)

After flying the Sea Hawk I went to the Fighter Development Unit. Later I instructed on Vampires, Venoms and Hunters. From the Hunter, I moved on to the Sea Vixen.

The only thing that took me aback was the cockpit. It was offset to the left of the centerline. It took a short while to get used to it, but at night when you were coming in to land, you needed to be on the centerline. Luckily there was a big division in the windscreen. If you got your head behind that and kept it absolutely in line with the deck or centerline, everything was tickety boo. If you were using it in the day-fighter role, your view to the right was a bit restricted and you would have to jack your seat up to get a better view.

You could do a comfortable four-hour flight with in-flight refueling in the Sea Vixen. The controls and instruments were easy to hand and there was nothing hidden. In the Sea Vixen we had full hydraulic flying controls, whereas in the Sea Hawk you only had powered aileron control. I thought the flight controls were absolutely beautiful. You had two hydraulic systems for the flying controls and there were two other systems for landing gear, flaps and wheel brakes. It was beautifully geared and the controls felt very, very nice at almost all speeds. It was nice at supersonic speeds, but at low speeds it could be just a little bit sluggish. You have to remember, it was a fairly large aircraft and we had to land at a very low speed in order to get onto our tiny little carriers.

The light fleet carriers that we had meant that it was crucial to get the right landing weight. Before you landed, you had to get your fuel down to the right amount. If anything went wrong, you'd have to go around. In that situation you went from burning or dumping fuel to frantically conserving what you had left!

I grew to love the Sea Vixen. It was big and strong, and I always felt very safe in the airplane. I had nearly 1,000 hours in that aircraft and at that time it was the most powerful airplane I had flown.

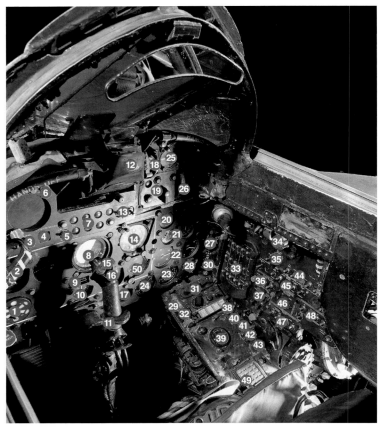

DE HAVILLAND
SEA VIXEN FAW MK 2
Fleet Air Arm Museum, Yeovilton, England

1. Red Top Ready Indicator
2. Hood Jettison Control
3. LABS Switch
4. Flight Refueling Indicator
5. Flight Refueling Receive Switch
6. LABS Indictor Light
7. Fuel Transfer Indicators
8. Attitude Indicator
9. Turn-and-Slip Indicator
10. Angle-of-Attack Indicator
11. Control Stick
12. Gunsight
13. Fuel Filter De-Icing Systems Switches
14. Gyro Compass
15. Tailplane/Aileron Trim Switch
16. Auto-Throttle Clutch Switch
17. Tailplane Trim Indicator
18. Autostabiliser Switches
19. Auto-Pilot Control Panel
20. JPT Gauges
21. RPM Gauges
22. Fuel Contents Gauges
23. Flowmeter
24. TACAN Indicator
25. Accelerometer
26. Auto-Pilot Elevon Position Indicator
27. PAS Armament Selector
28. Drop Tanks Fuel Transfer Indicators
29. Wing/Radome Locked Indicator
30. Cabin Pressure Altimeter
31. UHF Manual Channel Selector
32. Seat Height Adjustment Switch
33. Booster Pumps Switch Panel
34. Cabin Temp Selector
35. Fuel Jettison Switch
36. GW Switches
37. Heavy Stores Jettison Switches
38. Engine Master Switches
39. Oxygen Regulator
40. Ignition Switches
41. Battery Master Switch
42. Generator Isolation Switches
43. Engine Starter Push Buttons
44. External Light Switches
45. Radio Switch Bank
46. Master Armament Selector Switch
47. Bombs Switches
48. Rocket Switches
49. Standard Warning Panel
50. Artificial Horizon

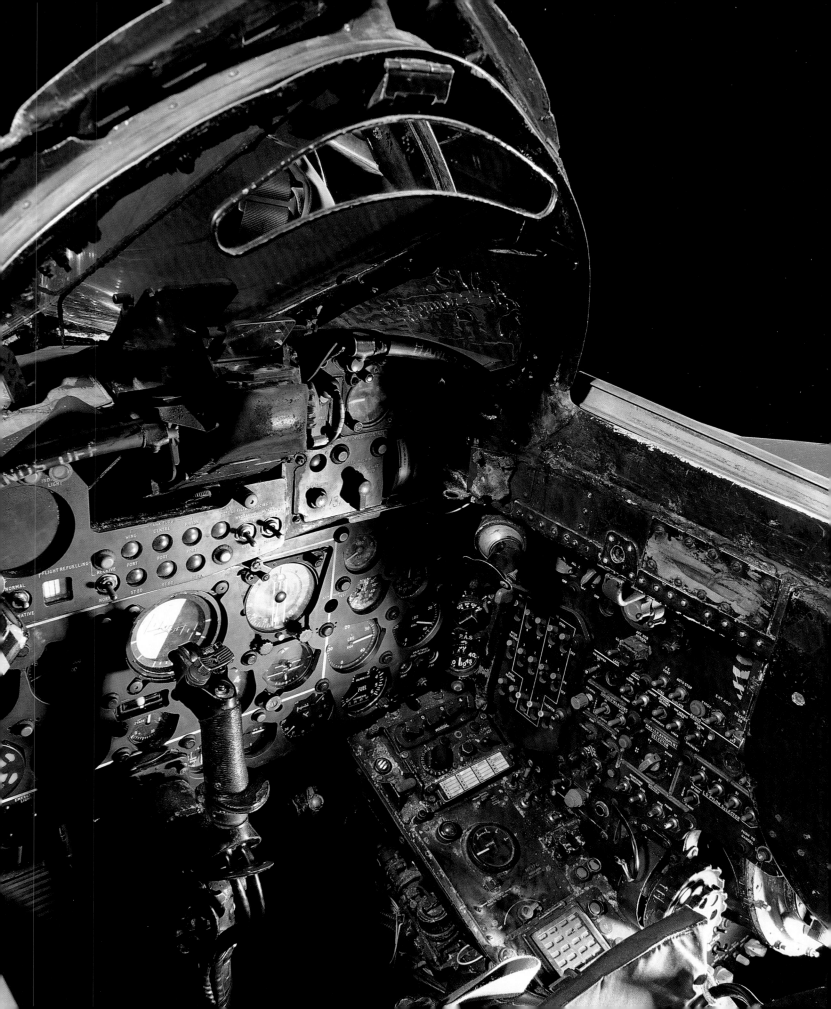

ENGLISH ELECTRIC
CANBERRA

CONSERVATIVE IN LAYOUT BUT NOT PERFORMANCE, THE STRAIGHT-WING CANBERRA
WAS ONE OF THE MOST SUCCESSFUL AND VERSATILE JET BOMBERS EVER BUILT!

By the middle of 1944, both the Gloster Meteor and de Havilland Vampire had shown that the jet engine was a viable form of aircraft propulsion. The Ministry of Aircraft Procurement quickly issued a specification calling for a new, fast, jet-powered medium bomber. Its piston-engine counterpart was the de Havilland Mosquito, which had proven itself during the Second World War as an outstanding medium bomber, fighter bomber and night fighter. The English Electric Aircraft Company, which had been building bombers and fighters under license since 1938, took up the challenge.

At the very beginning, the new Canberra was to be powered by a single jet engine developing 12,000 pounds (5,440 kg) of thrust. This idea was soon dropped because it would have meant a limited bomb load and fuel capacity. Eventually, a twin-engine, mid-wing layout with a streamlined fuselage and room for a pilot and navigator sitting side-by-side was adopted. The wing was straight and had a low aspect ratio. While it cut down on the speed of the aircraft, the wing area was so generous, it gave the Canberra an amazing rate of climb, excellent ceiling, the maneuverability of a fighter, and great operational flexibility. Powered by two wing-mounted Rolls-Royce Avon 109 engines, the prototype Canberra took to the air on May 13, 1949.

The first Canberra to reach RAF squadron service was the B.2 variant. This had a glazed nose for the navigator/bombardier. Just as the Canberra entered operational service, the Americans began show a keen interest in the new bomber. In 1951, the Canberra was displayed for U.S. officials in Washington and Baltimore. After this, a license-built B-57 version was built by Martin. The U.S. Canberra was equipped with two J65 engines and was capable of carrying 6,000 pounds (2,270 kg) of bombs internally and on sixteen underwing pylons. The two crew members sat one behind the other in a central cockpit. The B-57 served with the USAF from 1955 until 1964 and was used effectively as a light tactical bomber during the Vietnam War.

By 1954 there were eighteen Canberra squadrons in service with the RAF. It was soon realized that the speed and range of the Canberra made it an ideal candidate for the photo reconnaissance role. Soon the PR.3 appeared with a lengthened fuselage to accommodate seven cameras.

In 1956, the Canberra went to war with the RAF. With the seizure of the Suez Canal by Egyptian President Abdel Nasser, Britain and France immediately sent forces to the area and issued an ultimatum to the Egyptians. When no reply to the ultimatum was forthcoming, Canberras from Malta and Cyprus carried out their first bombing raids of the war.

Both the Canberra and B-57 proved a great success with air forces of nations around the world, including Argentina, Australia, Ecuador, Ethiopia, Germany, India, Pakistan, Peru, Rhodesia, South Africa, Sweden, Taiwan and Venezuela. In 1999, the Canberra celebrated fifty years of service in the Royal Air Force, a testament to its sound design and reliable performance. In total, 903 Canberras were built, including 403 B-57s built in the United States and 48 in Australia.

Above: This shot of a Canberra B.6 clearly shows its straight, broad wings, which provided for much of its outstanding performance. Right: A fine study of the first Canberra B.2. Between 1951 and 1958, the Canberra set twenty-two world records for distance in time and altitude.

PILOT'S PERSPECTIVE
Air Commodore P. J. Wilkinson
RAF (Ret.)

The basic Canberra gave the pilot a comfortable environment — seated on a Martin Baker "bang seat" under a goldfish-bowl canopy. Out of it you could see quite well from wingtip to wingtip, and well enough forward to make approach and landing a simple task. But visibility came with a price: comfort did not include the other environmental features. Both on the ground and in the air, the sun had vigorous effect, and it could get uncomfortably hot, especially since the air-conditioning system was patchy in its effect. But down below the canopy rim, where the sun didn't shine, the lower bits of the body suffered too, from lack of temperature: ineffective airframe insulation and low-quality air conditioning meant that a high-level sortie of any length resulted in very cold toes and hands.

The general cockpit and instrument panel followed the classic RAF pattern, and was adequate for the roles and missions of the standard aircraft, all those from B.2 and PR.3 to their successors and variants that used the original airframe shape, including the T.19. Those pilots who had the good fortune to have flown (or still be flying) the B.(I)8 or the PR.9 will all agree that those two developed versions marked a major

step forward in cockpit terms. Up on top, under a fighter-type canopy, the pilot had a much better view. Role equipment, for either bomber or reconnaissance version, and associated instruments, all had moved a step closer forward from the World War II feel of the early Canberras. The stick top, although still fixed on the right-hand element of a "spectacle," had all the "tits and knobs" that a fighter aircraft's single stick provided.

Nevertheless, the basic Canberra cockpit, as on the T.19, gave the pilot a relatively simple working environment and, with crew co-operation, the aircraft had all the potential to be an effective operational system. Fifty-plus years on, it is still called on, in the considerably developed PR.9 version, to realize that potential.

Above: A Canberra PR.3 poses for the camera during arrivals day at the 1953 SBAC Show at Farnborough.

ENGLISH ELECTRIC CANBERRA T.19
Newark Air Museum, Newark, England

1. Control Column
2. Wheel Brakes Lever
3. Cockpit Light
4. Undercarriage Emergency Control
5. Undercarriage Control Push Buttons
6. Alighting Gear Master Switch
7. Undercarriage Indicator
8. Flaps Selector Switch
9. Cockpit Lighting

10. Rudder Trim Indicator
11. Mach Meter
12. Tail Trim Indicator
13. Aileron Trim Indicator
14. Zero Reader Control Unit
15. Flaps Position Indicator
16. Engine Master Start Switches
17. No. 1 Engine Ignition Switch
18. No. 2 Engine Switch
19. No. 2 Engine Starter Push Switch

20. Compass Change Over Switch
21. Artificial Horizon
22. Rate-of-Climb Indicator
23. Gyro Compass
24. Turn-and-Slip Indicator
25. Turn-and-Slip Emergency Supply Switch
26. Tachometer
27. Jet Pipe Temp Gauge
28. Oil Pressure Gauge
29. Fuel Gauges

30. Fuel Pump Cock Switches
31. Engine Fuel Warning Light
32. Overload Tank Switch
33. Engine Fire Warning Push Switches
34. Cabin Pressure Warning Horn Override Switch
35. V/UHF Selector Switch
36. V/UHF Selector Switch
37. Cabin Altimeter
38. Hydraulic System Pressure Gauge

39. V/UHF Control Unit
40. Navigator's Oxygen Indicator
41. Cabin Pressure /Heat Indicator
42. Wheel Brakes Hydraulic Pressure Gauge
43. Passenger Oxygen Indicator
44. Cabin Pressure/Heat Control
45. ILS/TACAN Switch

VICKERS
VALIANT

ORIGINALLY DESIGNED AS A SIMPLE, INTERIM, NO-FRILLS BOMBER, THE VICKERS VALIANT ACCOMPLISHED
MANY FIRSTS AND PROVED TO BE A VERSATILE AND RELIABLE FIRST-GENERATION JET BOMBER.

In the wake of the most destructive and expensive war the world had ever seen, two inventions were to emerge that would change defense thinking for decades to follow — the jet engine and the atomic bomb. Near the end of World War II, the RAF began thinking of what would replace the Avro Lancaster, Lincoln and Handley Page Halifax bombers. The British had decided to develop their own atomic weapons and believed that nuclear deterrence was the best defense against nuclear attack. To pursue this policy, the RAF needed a bomber capable of carrying one 10,000-pound (4,535 kg) atomic bomb to a target 2,000 nautical miles away. It also had to attack targets deep in enemy territory without being destroyed by ground or air-launched missiles or intercepted by jet fighters. This required the new "V" bomber to fly as high as 40,000 feet with a speed close to 600 mph (965 km/h).

Three firms famous for their wartime bomber designs were the final serious contenders to build the new "V" bomber force. While Avro and Handley Page pursed the more advanced delta-wing and crescent-wing bomber designs, Vickers opted for a more simple swept-wing aircraft. After careful deliberation, the more advanced Avro Vulcan and Handley Page Victor were chosen, but just as the Vickers design was rejected, relations between the Soviet Union and her allies deteriorated. Suddenly, the Valiant was moved to the front of the line. Both the Vulcan and Victor first flew in 1952, but because of their more complicated wings and design they did not enter service until 1956 and 1957 respectively. The RAF needed to acquire their new bomber as soon as possible.

On May 18, 1951, the Valiant prototype took to the air. Sadly, on January 12, 1952, the first prototype crashed after catching fire at low altitude. The loss of the first prototype was a major setback, but the program continued with an order for 25 Valiant B.1s in April 1951. After the first 25 aircraft left the line, four further batches of 41, 56, 18 and 36 machines were ordered.

The first squadron to receive the Valiant was 138 Squadron on January 1, 1955. By 1957, there were eight squadrons equipped with the Valiant. Just as the RAF was forming new Valiant squadrons, Bomber Command suddenly found itself involved in preparations for a bombing campaign far from its home bases. In 1956, the Egyptian government made plans to nationalize the Suez Canal. The British and French reacted by sending naval, air and ground forces to the area. Four Valiant squadrons were assigned to the task. During the six-day period of operations, Valiants and Canberras flew 395 sorties, dropping 942 tons of bombs. The results were not good. Bomber Command was ill-prepared for this type of limited war. Ironically, the Valiants had to use World War II bombing methods in good weather to hit their targets.

By 1962, the introduction of the Mk 2 Vulcans and Victors was well underway and 138 Squadron became the first Valiant unit to disband.

The "interim" Vickers Valiant was a remarkable aircraft. It was the first and only RAF aircraft to have dropped live nuclear weapons, the first to fill the low-level bombing role and the first RAF tanker aircraft to enter service. By 1965, the last tanker Valiants were withdrawn from service. In the end, 104 Vickers Valiants were built.

Above: The all-black Valiant B.2 prototype was specially designed for the low-level bombing role but was never ordered.
Right: The Valiant was well liked by its crews. As a target of interception, the Valiant also earned
a healthy amount of respect from the pilots of Fighter Command.

PILOT'S PERSPECTIVE
Commodore Arthur Steele
RAF (Ret.)

After the small, compact Canberra, the Valiant seemed large and complex. Two pilots sat well above the two navigators and air electronics officer, who were in a somewhat dark hole facing the tail, with wall-to-wall navigation, bombing and communications equipment in front and the visual bombsight behind them.

Pilot ejector seats were comfortable enough for a few hours, but distinctly uncomfortable for an eight-hour mission. Rear crew members could stretch and move around but pilots were always aware of one concern — for the rear crew members, escape meant going out the side entrance door close to the engine-air intakes. We always hoped that an emergency bail-out situation would not arise.

Visibility forward and to the side was good and comfortable for formation flying, but rearward view was limited. Small, adjustable rearview mirrors fitted to side window frames gave some view beyond the wingtips for taxiing and flight. The flight and engine instruments were not fancy — a standard instrument panel, large easy-to-read dials and well-positioned controls for the undercarriage, flaps (nicknamed "barn doors") air brakes and engine fire-extinguisher buttons. The throttles were agricultural — long and with a large angular movement between idling and full power. But they worked obediently.

Fuel gauges and switches made it easy to manage the fuel system to keep the center of gravity and spanwise loading of the wings within limits. All in all, it was a straightforward and welcoming cockpit that, coupled to the splendid handling characteristics of the aircraft, made the Valiant a joy to fly as a bomber, tanker or reconnaissance aircraft.

Cockpit changes were made to eight special aircraft of 49 Squadron for British megaton weapons tests at Christmas Island in the Pacific in 1957/58. These included removable steel shutters to shield the crew from weapon flash effects, a sensitive accelerometer for the escape maneuver after weapon release, and modifications to the auto-pilot to permit safe escape in an emergency.

Wing-spar fatigue brought an end to the Valiant, but it proved it could fulfill any of the roles for which it was designed and stood proudly alongside its sister V bombers. It was a pleasure to be allowed to be part of such a splendid cockpit.

VICKERS VALIANT MK 2
Newark Air Museum, Newark, England

1. Elevator Trim Indicator Lights
2. ADF Bearing Compass
3. Port Landing Lamp Filament Switch
4. Starboard Landing Lamp Filament Switch
5. No. 1 Engine Master Cock Switch
6. No. 2 Engine Master Cock Switch
7. Fire-Extinguisher Pushbuttons
8. Fire-Extinguisher Warning Lights Push Button Port
9. Fire-Extinguisher Warning Lights Push Button Starboard
10. U/V Lamp Socket
11. Fuel Filter De-Icing Switch

12. Fuel Filter De-Icing Warning Lamp
13. No. 3 Engine Master Cock Switch
14. No. 4 Engine Master Cock Switch
15. Instrument Master Switch
16. Main Flap Motor Trip Button
17. Emergency Flap Motor Trip Button
18. Low Pressure Fuel Warning Lights
19. JPT Fuel Control Switch
20. Port Pressure Head Heater Switch
21. Oxygen Remote Blinker Indicator

22. Airspeed Indicator
23. Artificial Horizon
24. Rate-of-Climb Indicator
25. G.4B Compass Indicator
26. Turn-and-Slip Indicator
27. Brake Pressure Gauge
28. Bombing Direction Indicator
29. JPT Gauges
30. RPM Indicators
31. Throttle Levers
32. Oil Pressure Gauges
33. Oil Temp Gauge
34. Volt Meter
35. Tailplane Incidence Indicator
36. Port Flap Position Indicator

37. Starboard Flap Position Indicator
38. Altimeter
39. Oxygen Remote Blinker Indicator
40. Rate-of-Climb Indicator
41. Starbord Pressure Head Heater Switch
42. Low Level Radio Altimeter Limit Lights
43. Rudder Feel Unit Cut-Off Lever
44. Feel Units Trimming Switch
45. Throttle Friction Lever
46. Aileron Feel Unit Cut-Off Lever
47. Elevator Feel Cut-Off Lever
48. Bomb Door Control Switch

49. Tailplane Incident Switch
50. Flap Emergency Selector Switch
51. Tailplane Incidence Switch
52. RATOG Master Switch
53. Auto-Pilot Controller
54. RATOG Normal Release Switch
55. Bomb Jettison Switch
56. Internal Control Locks Lever
57. Undercarriage Down Selector Button
58. Under Carriage Emergency Down Selector Button
59. Fuel Tank Pressure Gauge

AVRO

VULCAN

CONCEIVED IN 1947 AND FIRST SHOWN AT FARNBOROUGH, THE HUGE DELTA-WING
AVRO VULCAN WOULD BECOME BRITAIN'S MOST RECOGNIZABLE NUCLEAR DETERRENT
AND A FAVORITE AT AIR SHOWS AROUND THE WORLD.

By the end of the Second World War, Britain and the United States had spent huge sums building and maintaining powerful strategic-bomber fleets. These forces completely devastated Germany and Japan, and with the introduction of the atomic bomb, it was now possible to send a single aircraft to destroy a city, a task that previously required a thousand or more aircraft. In conjunction with the advent of the A-bomb, the development of jet technology meant that attacking aircraft could now fly twice as fast and twice as high as previous piston-engine aircraft. In this new and threatening environment, the Air Ministry issued Specification B.35/46, calling for a bomber capable of carrying a 10,000-pound (4,540 kg) nuclear bomb for over 3,000 miles (4,830 km) at over 600 mph (965 km/h), with an over-the-target height of 50,000 feet.

The new specifications were daunting and some aircraft companies did not think it possible, but there were two that did — Handley Page and Avro. Both companies submitted very advanced designs that would require much testing and development. In case these two designs did not pan out, the RAF instructed Vickers to build a more conventional aircraft, which became the Valiant.

Avro pressed ahead and created a dramatically new aircraft. When the first Vulcan appeared, its tailless delta shape was truly inspired. The thick, massive wing enabled the four engines to be buried deep inside the aircraft and allowed for an ample fuel load. The crew consisted of five members: pilot, co-pilot, nav-radar, nav-plotter and AEO (air electronics officer). All were housed in a double-deck pressurized compartment, but only the pilot and co-pilot had ejection seats. On

August 31, 1952, the first flight of the Vulcan took place, but it was not until January 1957 that the first Operational Conversion Unit received it first Vulcan.

The first Vulcan to see service was the B.1 version. These were powered by four Olympus turbojets each producing 11,000 pounds (5,000 kg) of thrust and had the original straight leading-edge wing. This was quickly modified with a drooped and kinked leading edge, which improved performance at high altitude. The next major variant was the B.2, equipped with more powerful engines and the ability to carry the new Blue Steel cruise missile. The B.2 served with 9, 12, 27, 35, 44, 50, 83, 101 and 617 Squadrons and, along with the Valiant and Victor squadrons, provided Britain with its V-Force — Britain's nuclear deterrent during the early years of the Cold War. Beginning in 1963, the Vulcan force was withdrawn from the high-level nuclear strike role and began training for low-level nuclear delivery and tactical bombing. Painted gray-green and capable of carrying nuclear weapons or twenty-one 1,000 pound (455 kg) bombs, the Vulcan was expected to operate at 500 feet or less in order to avoid enemy missiles and anti-aircraft fire.

Planned withdrawal for the Vulcan was scheduled for between June 1981 and June 1982, but in April 1982 the Falklands War thrust the few remaining Vulcans into combat for the first and last time. Flying the longest bombing missions in the history of air warfare, Vulcans made five "Black Buck" missions (two bombing, three anti-radar strikes) from Ascension Island to Port Stanley and back. Round trip — 8,000 miles (12,870 km). During the Falklands War, six Vulcans were converted to K.2A aerial tankers and served in that role until March 1984. There were 134 Vulcans built.

Left: Rarely seen in formation, these three Waddington-based Vulcans strike an ominous pose. The white gloss finish was designed to be able to withstand over 70 calories of energy per square centimeter from a nuclear blast. Above: The back end of a Vulcan B.2.

PILOT'S PERSPECTIVE
Air Vice-Marshal Ron Dick
RAF (Ret.)

The cockpit of the Vulcan 2 was cramped and claustrophobic. The two pilots were squeezed onto an upper deck originally intended for one, and the three rear crew members (electronics, nav-plotter, nav radar) sat elbow to elbow on a dark lower flight deck. The pilots had minimal windows to the front and small portholes to the side, all provided with screens to shield the crew's eyes from nuclear flash during the ultimate high-level operational sortie. Once the wartime mission became low level in 1962, the Vulcan could not be flown blacked out, so one pilot's screen was left open and he wore a patch over one eye. One flash — shift the patch. Two flashes — hand over to the co-pilot. Four nuclear flashes could be absorbed before the pilots were out of eyes.

Apart from this alarming novelty, arrangements in the Vulcan cockpit were relatively conventional. Standard instrument panels faced each of the pilots and rows of engine instruments were between the two. Across the top was a string of warning lights and indicators to alert the pilots to multifarious emergencies, and above them, strongly marked in black and yellow, were the engine fire lights and extinguisher buttons and the T-handle for extending the ram air turbine (RAT). Centrally placed below the warning lights were the control surfaces position indicator (a visual representation of how the eight elevons and the rudder were moving), the military flight system selector, the split switch for streaming/jettisoning the brake parachute, and the auto-pilot trim indicator. To the left of the CSPI was a small but important instrument: the G meter. Designed principally to fly at high altitude in straight lines, the Vulcan would not tolerate high-stress maneuvers: its limit was just 2G.

Between the seats, a central quadrant housed four throttle levers with relight buttons in their tops. An air-brake switch was just behind the throttles, and underneath was a retractable fuel-system tray with an array of booster pumps normally supplying automatically sequenced flow from fourteen fuel tanks. Unusual in such a large aircraft were identical fighter-type control sticks, each with a "coolie hat" trim switch and buttons for radio and intercom transmissions, artificial feel relief, nosewheel steering, and auto-pilot cut-out.

The most disturbing feature of the Vulcan crew compartment was its "us and them" character. The pilots had ejection seats; the rear crew did not.

AVRO VULCAN B MK 2
Newark Air Museum, Newark, England

1. Ram Air Turbine Release Handle
2. Engine Fire Indicator/ Operating Switches
3. HTP Tank Temp Warning
4. Store Fire Warning
5. Store Fire Warning
6. ILS Marker Lamp
7. Main Warning Systems Indicators
8. PFC Unit Failure Indicator
9. Artificial Feel Failure Indicator
10. Auto Stabilizers Indicator
11. Air Brakes Indicator
12. Bomb Door Position Indicator
13. Alternator Failure Indicator
14. Canopy Unlocked Indicator
15. Entrance Door Unlocked Indicator
16. Pitot Heater Indicator
17. Main Warning Systems Indicators
18. TFR Warning Indicator
19. Fuel Fire Bomb Bay Tanks Warning Indicator
20. Fuel Fire Fuselage/ Wing Tank Warning Indicator
21. ILS Marker Lamp
22. Artificial Feel Relief Cut-out Switch
23. Elevon Trim
24. Intercom Switch
25. Mach Meter
26. Accelerometer
27. Control Surface Indicator
28. MFS Selector Unit
29. Selected Altitude Indicator Lamps
30. TFR Reset Button
31. Mach Meter
32. Director Horizon
33. Rate-of-Climb Indicator
34. Engine Temp Indicators
35. Tail Parachute Control
36. Auto-pilot Trim Indicator
37. Air Speed Indicator
38. Director Horizon
39. Climb and Descent Indicator
40. Fuel Low Pressure Warning Indicators
41. RPM Governor Indicator
42. Engine RPM Indicators
43. Throttle Controls
44. Oil Pressure Gauges
45. RPM Governor Switch
46. Throttle Friction Adjuster
47. Control Handle
48. Beam Compass
49. Artificial Horizon
50. Bombing Indicator
51. Rudder Pedal Adjuster
52. Jet Pipe Temp Limiter Switch
53. Auto Throttle Engage Switch
54. Air Brakes Selector Switch
55. 10,000 ft-Altimeter
56. ADF Bearing Compass
57. Beam Compass
58. Total Fuel Flow Indicator
59. Fuel Flow Indicator Switch
60. Intercom Control Unit
61. Auto-pilot Control
62. Emergency Trim Control
63. Fuel System Control Panel
64. Red Flood Lamps
65. Bomb Bay Tanks System Control
66. Windscreen Wiper Switches

<small>HANDLEY PAGE</small>

VICTOR

<small>THE LAST OF THE V-BOMBERS TO ENTER SERVICE, THE VICTOR WAS ALSO THE LAST IN A LONG LINE OF FAMOUS HANDLEY BOMBERS THAT BEGAN IN 1918 WITH THE TWIN-ENGINE OPEN-COCKPIT O/400.</small>

The most distinctive and recognizable feature of the futuristic-looking Victor was its remarkable crescent wing. This design feature came out of the same B.35/46 specification for which the Vulcan was envisioned. The unique crescent-wing platform allowed for a constant critical Mach number to be maintained from the wing root to the tip of the wing, for improved performance at all altitudes.

In 1947, design work began on the H.P.80. This prototype flew for the first time on December 24, 1952, but was lost on July 14, 1954, due to fatigue failure and loss of the tailplane during a low-level run. A second prototype flew in September 1954, and was followed by the first production Victor B Mk 1 in February 1956.

Compared to the Vulcan and Valiant, the Victor had a much larger bomb bay (35,000 pounds, compared to 21,000 pounds for the Vulcan [15,875 kg; 9,525 kg]) and a very different crew compartment. In the Victor, the five crew members were seated together in one compartment and not separated as in the Vulcan and Valiant. Powered by four 11,000-pound-thrust (4,990 kg) Bristol Siddeley Sapphire jet engines, the Victor B Mk 1 could fly at speeds just under Mach 1 at altitudes between 40,000 and 50,000 feet with an unrefueled flight range at altitude of some 4,000 miles (6,435 km). On June 1, 1957, the first production Victor broke the sound barrier during a shallow dive from 40,000 feet during a delivery flight to 232 Operational Conversion Unit. At the time, it was the largest aircraft in the world to exceed Mach 1! Bomber Command became operational with the Victor in April 1958 with 10 Squadron. The total force of four Victor B Mk 1 squadrons was completed by 1960. No. 534 Squadron also received the reconnaissance version of the Victor.

The final bomber version of the Victor to see service was the B Mk 2. Externally, the Mk 2 was similar in appearance to the Mk 1, but internally, the Mk 2 was equipped with four Rolls-Royce Conway turbojets rated at 20,000 pounds (9,070 kg) of thrust. This was almost twice the thrust available to the Victor B Mk 1. The new engines required the redesign of the wing roots, intakes and engine boxes, along with an extended wingspan. The first B Mk 2 flew on February 1959. Ironically, the improved high-altitude performance of the B Mk 2 was never to be realized. In the early 1960s the threat of intercontinental ballistic missiles had grown tremendously, and the improvement of Soviet air defenses spelled the end of high-level penetration of Soviet air space. The Victor, along with the Vulcan and Valiant, was switched to the low-level bombing role. Green and gray camouflage replaced the earlier anti-flash white, and the Victor began carrying the Blue Steel nuclear missile. As the B Mk 2 started to replace the B Mk 1s, they in turn were being converted to three-point refueling tankers. Four squadrons, 55, 57, 214 and 19, would serve in the air-to-air refueling role. By the early 1980s there were only twenty-four Victors left in the air-tanker role, but in 1982 they would perform their greatest missions. The Argentine invasion of the Falkland Islands in 1982 would push the entire Victor tanker to the extreme limits of their capability. In the famous Vulcan Black Buck mission, Victor tankers (eleven for each mission) had to refuel a single Vulcan and each other from Ascension Island to the Falklands and back. It was an incredible feat of arms and one that has never been repeated. In 1990, the Victor tanker force was once again called into action. The Gulf War saw eight Victors from 55 Squadron fly 299 sorties, refueling RAF, U.S. Navy and other coalition aircraft. In 1993, the Victor tanker was finally retired.

Left: A Victor K Mk 2 from 55 Squadron on one of its last flights before the end of its operational life in 1993.

PILOT'S PERSPECTIVE
Air Commodore Arthur Steele
RAF (Ret.)

I needed to qualify on the Victor to become chief instructor at the Operational Conversion Unit (OCU) at Gaydon, England, which trained crews on Valiants and Victors. My first impression of the needle-nosed, high-tailplane Victor cockpit was that it was well laid out and functional. As an integrated cockpit, it was less claustrophobic than the Valiant for the two navigators and air electronics officer in the back since the rear deck was slightly higher than the pilot station. Communication between the five crew members was easier, including when it came to dispensing hot soup on long flights. As in the other V-bombers, only the pilots had ejection seats, and the rear crew members had to escape through the entrance door in an emergency.

There were no major problems about the cockpit layout. Fuel control switches and gauges were easy to reach, but the fuel system was slightly more complex than the Valiant, especially with two engines out on the same side. But there was nothing unmanageable about it. One slight trap for pilots in the main system concerned the wheel brakes. Brake pedals were situated just above the main rudder pedals, and it was possible to have partial braking pressure applied on touchdown, which led to several multiple tire bursts and embarrassment all round. So the final landing check was "feet off the brakes"!

Visibility from the Victor was good, and even the rear crew members could see something of was going on in front just by turning their heads. The workload in the Victor was basically the same as the Valiant, since they had the same fundamental nav/attack and communications systems.

I suppose the thing I liked least about the cockpit was the location, initially, of the braking-parachute selector switch, which sat rather out of the way on the lower left-hand coaming. The pilot really had to glance at it before touchdown to make sure of hitting the right switch at the right time — an unwelcome complication when landing on a short runway in a crosswind. The switch was relocated to a better position later.

Overall, the Victor cockpit was accessible and functional and enabled the crew to provide a sound platform for bombing, tanker and strategic reconnaissance operations. And the Victor had the final say by providing essential tanker capacity long after the Valiant and Vulcan ceased operations.

HANDLEY PAGE VICTOR K MK 2
British Aviation Heritage, Bruntingthorpe, England

1. Fire Warning Test Warning Lamps
2. Brake Parachute Switches
3. Clock
4. Out-of-Trim Indicator
5. Auto Trim Warning Light
6. Auto Stabilizer Control
7. Machmeter
8. Gyro Compass
9. Emergency Hydraulic Warning Light
10. Panel Dimmer Switch
11. Airspeed Indicator
12. Rate-of-Climb Indicator
13. Flaps Position Indicator

14. Air Brake Indicator
15. Director Horizon
16. Beam Compass
17. Turn-and-Slip Indicator
18. Yaw, Roll, Pitch Indicators
19. Accelerometer
20. Nose Flap Warning Indicators & High Intensity Light Switch
21. Altimeter
22. Artificial Horizon
23. Nose Steering Handwheel
24. Low Pressure Warning Lights
25. Emergency Hydraulics Warning Lights
26. Pitot Heaters

27. Tachometers
28. Engine Exhaust Temp Gauges
29. Oil Pressure Gauges
30. Wing & Fuselage Fuel Gauges
31. Wing Pump Switches
32. Fuel Feed Indicators
33. Fuel Cock Switches
34. Fuselage Pump Switches
35. Bomb Bay Fuel Pump Switches
36. Military Flight System Selector
37. Auto-pilot Master Switches
38. Dimmer Switches
39. Internal Engine Fire Warning Lights

40. Engine Bay Fire Warning Lights
41. Power Flying Control Switches and Warning Lights
42. Landing Gear Selector
43. Flaps Selector and Emergency Flaps Down Switch
44. Wing Fire Warning Lights
45. Fuselage Warning Lights
46. Landing Gear Indicator Lights
47. Mach Trim Switch and Indicator
48. Auto Trim Switch & Indicator
49. Auto-pilot Indicator
50. Panel Dimmer Switch
51. JPT Control

52. De-Ice and Overheat Switch and Indicator
53. Pattern Speed Indicator
54. Annunciator Unit
55. Windscreen Demisting Control
56. Engine Air Bleed Valves Indicators
57. Out of Trim Indicator
58. Tail and Nose Heavy Trim Indicator
59. Outside Air Temp
60. Control Column
61. Engine Start Controls
62. Brake Supply Gauges
63. Auto-pilot

BUCCANEER

THE BUCCANEER WAS AN IMMENSELY STRONG AND MANEUVERABLE AIRCRAFT.
ITS LOW-LEVEL SPEED, RANGE AND WEAPONS-CARRYING ABILITY PROVED BETTER
THAN THOSE OF THE F-111 AND THE TORNADO, THE AIRCRAFT DESIGNED TO REPLACE IT.

At the height of the Cold War, the Soviets introduced their new "Sverdlov" class heavy cruiser. These new, heavily armed cruisers displaced a staggering 17,000 tons with a speed of 34 knots. This posed a serious threat to Britain's merchant-shipping lanes. To counter the new Soviet threat, the Royal Navy's Air Warfare Division suggested the Fleet Air Arm be equipped with a new strike aircraft capable of carrying a nuclear weapon at high speed and ultra-low level. Pinpoint bombing accuracy was not required because one nuclear bomb would have been more than enough to destroy any one of the new Soviet cruisers.

In 1953, the Naval Staff Requirement NA.39 was issued. Blackburn Aircraft won the tender to produce the aircraft and began work on one of the most advanced naval strike aircraft ever designed. To meet the Royal Navy's demand for an aircraft to fly at low level and high speed, Blackburn had to introduce new construction and design techniques. These techniques were kept secret well into 1957. The initial design for the Buccaneer was completed in July 1954 and a development contract for 20 pre-production aircraft was placed. The first Buccaneer prototype flew on April 30, 1958. Carrier trials soon followed, and in January 1960, the Buccaneer made it first landing on the HMS *Victorious*.

The first squadron to be equipped with the new Buccaneer was 700Z. The trials squadron's task was to get the new aircraft into service as soon as possible. In 1961, the new Buccaneers were painted with anti-flash white for its nuclear strike role. One of the unique features of the Buccaneer was its revolving bomb bay. Weapons could be carried internally, thus eliminating the need for drag-inducing bomb-bay doors.

The first combat-ready Buccaneers became operational with 801 Squadron, when they received their first Buccaneer Mk 1s in July 1962. Operations in hot-weather climates revealed the new aircraft's short comings. The Mk 1's Gyron Junior engines were not powerful enough to get a fully loaded Buccaneer off the deck. In order to take off with a full weapons load, the Buccaneer would be launched with a light fuel load and be refueled immediately in the air with a Scimitar aerial tanker. To address the power problems, the Rolls-Royce Spey engine (11,100 pounds/5,035 kg thrust) was chosen to power the new Mk 2 Buccaneer. The new Mk 2 was easily distinguished from the Mk 1 by the much larger air intakes.

In 1966, the British Labour Government canceled the navy's new carrier program and set the dates for the decommissioning of the remaining two carriers in service. Ironically and fortunately for the Buccaneer, the RAF's TRS.2 strike aircraft was also canceled. Grudgingly the RAF adopted the Buccaneer. With the RAF, the Buccaneer proved itself one of the world's finest low-level strike aircraft ever produced. It was the first time in history a Fleet Air Arm aircraft was adopted by the RAF. During the Gulf War, twelve Buccaneers provided laser designation for Tornado bombers. Buccaneers flew 216 sorties, dropping forty-eight laser-guided bombs.

In March 1994, the Buccaneer was finally retired from RAF service. To the end, the Buccaneer remained a potent aircraft and was in many respects better than the Tornado designed to replace it.

Left: A fine tribute to the Buccaneer. Seven Bucs pose for the camera in the many different color schemes it wore during its long career with the Fleet Air Arm and RAF.

PILOT'S PERSPECTIVE
Air Commodore P. J. Wilkinson
RAF (Ret.)

After sixteen years in the RAF and almost 3,000 hours of cockpit time, a double challenge. First, return to the cockpit after taking a long ground tour and transition on to the Buccaneer. Second, having got the first few clues on how to handle this complex aircraft, immediately take command of the Operational Conversion Unit (237 OCU) at RAF Honington, in Suffolk, and also function as chief instructor. With that agenda, I needed every possible boost to confidence in my own abilities. Unfortunately, the full-motion flight simulator seemed able only to remove any self-confidence I once had. The wretched device was so unresponsive of the Buccaneer approach and landing configurations and so peculiarly geared, that I failed to make a single successful simulated landing. How my unfortunate USAF back-seater felt about the consistent crashes, he was gentleman enough not to say! But my first flight in the real thing removed all doubts and brought great happiness.

The "Bucc" cockpit is known as an ergonomic slum: many quite important instruments are scattered in random fashion in different corners of the capacious cockpit. Some must be looked for more or less under the left elbow, while keeping the other eye on the head-up display on the right of the coaming. Never mind fly the bloody thing! And, to be honest, in approach configuration, with all lift-enhancing surfaces and associated air bleeds working, air brakes out and throttles pumping, it's a real handful. But at low (very low) level, and at sensible speeds for maneuver of 480 knots plus, it is a dream machine. Noise levels are high, although with modern headgear not impossible to work with. The view out of the canopy, above and behind, and forward visibility through the front screen — all very good, not hindered by the refueling probe. Indeed, the probe is very useful as a guide to bank angles when maneuvering at low level — never a good time to be looking inside for instruments readings. But the supreme feature of the "Banana Bomber" is ride quality: unsurpassed in my experience. You feel the air just being pushed aside; the whole thing feels like a roller-coaster car, swaying a little from side to side on its rails, but changing direction with brutal strength and answering every demand the pilot can place on it. Sadly, I had but the one tour of three years on the Bucc, but I'd love to have it all over again.

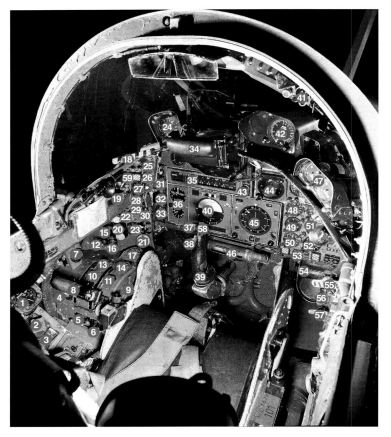

BLACKBURN BUCCANEER S MK 2B
Fleet Air Arm Museum, Yeovilton, England

1. Wheel Brakes Pressure Gauge
2. Rudder and Aileron Trim Control
3. Standby Tail Plane Trim Switch
4. Cameras Master Control Switch
5. Armament Supply Selector Switches
6. Bomb Door Selector Switch
7. Cabin Altimeter
8. Combined Throttle Controls
9. Throttle Lever Damping Control
10. Auto-pilot Engage Push Button
11. Bomb Door Position Indicator
12. AC Generator Control Switches
13. Wheel Brakes Anti-Skid Selector Switch
14. Aileron and Rudder Trim Indicators
15. Air Brakes Standby Switch
16. Battery Master Switch
17. Tail Plane Position Indicator
18. Canopy Jettison Control Handle
19. Attention Warning Lamps
20. Undercarriage Push Button Selector
21. Undercarriage Indicator
22. Landing and Taxiing Lamp Selector
23. Main Plane Flaps and Aileron Selector Controls
24. Deck Landing Air Speed Indicator
25. Cabin Anti-Dazzle Light Master Switch
26. Tail Plane Flap Position Indicator
27. Flaps and Aileron Drop Position Indicator
28. Stores Jettison Button
29. Arresting Hook Indicator Lamp
30. Arresting Hook Selector Switch
31. Compass Card Locking Switch
32. Attitude Indicator Fast Erection Switch
33. Oxygen Flow Indicators
34. Strike Site Display Unit
35. Airspeed Indicator and Mach Meter
36. Altimeter and Rate-of-Climb Indicators
37. Auto-pilot Instinctive Cut-out Push Button
38. Tail-Plane Trim Switch
39. Control Column
40. Attitude Indicator
41. Radio Altimeter Limit Lights
42. Radio Altimeter
43. Undercarriage Warning Lamp
44. Standby Artificial Horizon
45. Navigation Display
46. Adjustable Air Conditioning Nozzle
47. Wing Blowing System Pressure Gauges
48. High Pressure Shaft Speed Indicator
49. Turbine Gas Temp Indicators
50. Low Pressure Shaft Speed Indicators
51. Turbine Gas Temp Indicator
52. Low Pressure Shaft Speed Indicator
53. Engine Oil Pressure Indicators
54. Rudder Pedal
55. Windscreen Emergency De-Misting Control
56. Fuel/No-Air Valve Override Switches
57. Emergency Wheel Braking and Parking Handle
58. Weapons Release Trigger Safety Catch
59. Blowing System Indicators

FRANCE

DASSAULT
MYSTÈRE

MYSTÈRE

OFTEN OVERSHADOWED BY THE HUGELY SUCCESSFUL MIRAGE III,
THE DASSAULT MYSTÈRE WAS ONE OF EUROPE'S FINEST FIGHTERS AND
THE FIRST FRENCH FIGHTER TO EXCEED MACH 1 IN A DIVE.

The origins of the Mystère begin with Dassault's first fighter, the Ouragan. The Ouragan was a small straight-wing fighter similar to the Republic F-84. The prototype was powered by a single Rolls-Royce Nene engine of 5,000 pounds (2,270 kg) thrust, giving it a speed close to 600 mph (900 km/h). Even before the first prototype was delivered, the French government ordered 150 examples of the fighter in late August 1950. The Ouragan did not last long with the Armée de l'Air and was phased out in the spring of 1955. But even before the Ouragan saw service, Dassault was working on a more advanced machine.

The first Mystère was basically an Ouragan with 30-degree swept-wing and modified tail surfaces. Three Mystère I prototypes were built, and they were followed by two Mystère IIAs and then four Mystère IIBs. Eleven production prototypes were ordered and designated Mystère IICs. The speed of the Mystère IIC climbed to 660 mph (1,060 km/h) powered by a single SNECMA Atar turbojet rated at 5,510 pounds (2,500 kg) of thrust.

The promise of the new fighter was evident and Armée de l'Air ordered 150 Mystère IICs, The first production aircraft took to the air in June 1954. Armed with two 30 mm DEFA cannon, the Mystère IIC was one of Europe's most potent fighters. Fighter design in the 1950s moved at a phenomenal rate, and by 1957, when the last Mystère IIC was delivered, it was already being phased out.

The new Mystère IV was more a new design than a simple modification of the Mystère II. The new fighter had a more robust, oval section fuselage, a much thinner wing with increased sweep, and new tail surfaces. One prototype was ordered, followed by a contract for 225 Mystère IVs. The new fighter entered service in 1955 as an interceptor, but it would also be used in the ground-attack role. The Mystère IV first saw combat with the Israeli Air Force during the Suez Crisis in April 1956, and then again during the war in October. In both conflicts the Mystère proved itself more than a match against the MiG-15, and during the Six Day War in 1967, the Israelis still had two squadrons of Mystère IVs in service.

The last of the Ouragan/Mystère series to see active service was the "Super Mystère." The new Mystère in many ways resembled the F-100 Super Sabre. With its F-100-like oval air intake and 45-degree swept-back wings, the new Mystère had similar capabilities, but in a much smaller package. The Armée de l'Air ordered 180 Super Mystère B2s. The last of these were delivered in 1959. By this time, the Mirage III interceptor was just entering service and the Mystère B2 was relegated to the attack role, but it remained in service until 1977, when it was finally replaced by the Mirage IIIC and Mirage F1C fighters. The Israelis ordered thirty-six Super Mystères and used them to great effect during the Six Day War and the 1973 Yom Kippur War. In both conflicts the Super Mystère proved a match for the Soviet MiG-19.

In 1977, twelve ex-Israeli Super Mystères were sold to the Honduran Air Force, and there they served until 1989. All told, there were 577 Mystères built, serving with the air forces of France, India and Israel.

Above: Fighting in three wars with the Israeli Air Force and Indian Air Force, the Mystère IV proved a robust and capable fighter. Right: A lineup of Mystère IVs. In its last role as an advanced trainer, the Mystère gave hundreds of young pilots their first taste of supersonic flight.

PILOT'S PERSPECTIVE
Major General Daniel Bastien
Armée de l'Air

When I first flew the Mystère IV in 1975, it was no longer being used as a fighter but as an advanced trainer. After getting my wings in the T-33 T-Bird, I continued my training flying the Mystère IV. Our main mission was to perfect our air-combat skills and learn how to fly a fighter equipped with guns. We trained for both air-to-air and air-to-ground missions. For young pilots, the Mystère was a big step up from the T-Bird, and on our first flight we all went supersonic — the Mystère could go supersonic in a shallow dive. It was one of the most amazing days of my life. In those days we didn't have simulators and there was no two-seat version of the Mystère. We spent two weeks reading the book and then we were off! It was very exhilarating.

I found the Mystère cockpit very similar to the T-Bird's. It was a comfortable cockpit and pretty wide — wider than the Mirage III and Mirage F1, and even the Mirage 2000, which I flew much later. Visibility from the Mystère IV was good, but not great. I found the controls and instruments easy to reach and well placed. But there was a design problem. There were two control levers that were very close to each other — one was for flaps down and the other was for engine cut-off. As a consequence of this design problem, a few young pilots, instead of lowering their flaps when approaching their final turn, shut the engine off. Of course, it was too late to re-start the engine, and the pilots had to eject. You also had to be careful when flying a ground-attack mission. After diving on the target, you had to be careful when pulling out. If you did it too quickly, you would stall the aircraft. You also had to be vigilant with the throttle when flying high-altitude air-to-air combat. If you pushed it forward too quickly, the engine would flame out.

The Mystère was a beautiful aircraft, especially when you flew in close formation.

DASSAULT MYSTÈRE IVA
Imperial War Museum, Duxford, England

1. Locking Lever
2. Cockpit Light
3. UV Lights Rheostat
4. Canopy Controller Reverser
5. Light Switch
6. Red Lights Rheostat
7. Warning Horn Switch
8. Warning Horn Test Button
9. Parking Brake Handle
10. Accelerometer
11. Fuel Indicator Light
12. Fuel Treble Receptacle
13. Landing Gear Commutator
14. Throttle
15. Fuel Transfer Stop Button

16. Horizontal Stabilizer Emergency Control
17. Fuel Cock Control Lever
18. Gunsight
19. Master Battery Switch
20. Tachometer
21. Fuel Transfer Stop Button
22. Fuel Gauge
23. Control Stick
24. Airspeed Indicator
25. Altimeter
26. Radio Compass
27. Dimmer Selector
28. Jettisoning Switch
29. Artificial Horizon
30. Gyro Compass
31. Rudder Pedal Setting Handle
32. Cabin Altimeter

33. Rate-of-Climb Indicator
34. Slip-and-Turn Indicator
35. Run-up Unlocking Switch Light
36. Dual Receptacle
37. Landing Gear Control Board
38. Servo Pressure Indicator and Emergency Servo Control Indicator
39. VHF.2 Control Box
40. Shot Counter
41. Rocket Firing Box
42. Oxygen Warning Light
43. Emergency Servo Control Indicator Lamp
44. Run-Up Unlocking Switch
45. Emergency Pressurization Reverser
46. Electrical Panel

Left: The last of the Mystère series was the Super Mystère. Some 180 Super Mystères were built for the Armée de l'Air and remained in service until 1977.

SWEDEN

SAAB J 29 TUNNAN   SAAB J 32 LANSEN   SAAB J 35 DRAKEN

SAAB

J 29 TUNNAN

DESPITE ITS SMALL SIZE AND NEUTRAL STANCE, SWEDEN HAS PRODUCED
SOME OF THE WORLD'S MOST ADVANCED FIGHTERS — STARTING WITH
THE ROTUND J 29, EUROPE'S FIRST SWEPT-WING FIGHTER.

By the end of the Second World War, jet fighter design and development was growing exponentially. The first three generations of fighters on both sides of the Iron Curtain were designed primarily for air defense against bombers and not for the fighter-versus-fighter air-superiority role. Hiroshima and Nagasaki had clearly shown the world what a single bomber could do. In response to the new threat, the Swedish Air Board invited Saab to submit a proposal for a new jet fighter in the autumn of 1945.

Incredibly, with no previous jet experience, the Saab company was asked to produce a new fighter capable of high speeds (Mach 0.85-.86) a high service ceiling, excellent maneuverability, rugged construction, and armed with four 20 mm cannon. In the beginning a straight-wing configuration was favored, but in November 1945, Saab managed to obtain German aerodynamic research work that dealt directly with swept-wing outlining. A completely new wing was designed and, after testing, using a modified Saab Safir piston-engine trainer with a swept wing of 25 degrees, it became clear that the new fighter could achieve 620 mph (1,000 km/h).

In autumn 1946, three prototypes of the new J 29 were ordered. The new fighter was given a barrel-like shape with a central air intake in the nose and a straight air duct to the engine in the rear of the fuselage. The portly shape gave rise to the nickname "The Flying Barrel." With its large fuselage, the J 29 was able to carry 308 Imperial gallons (1,400 L) of fuel and an additional 154 gallons (700 L) in the wings and two 99-gallon (450 L) drop tanks. Compared to the North American F-86 Sabre, which carried a normal internal load of 362 gallons (1,646 L), the J 29 had 484 gallons (2,200 L) to burn. Powered by a de Havilland Ghost turbo jet of 5,000-pound (2,270 kg) thrust, the new J 29 was not only the first swept-wing fighter in Europe, it was also the first to have an all-movable tailplane, automatic leading-edge slats, full-span ailerons and a completely new Saab-designed ejection seat.

On September 1, 1948, the first flight of the J 29 took place. As with all new aircraft, unforeseen problems did arise. When the aircraft was pushed to Mach 0.8, directional snaking led to a Dutch roll that could not be controlled. This was soon remedied, and on February 29, 1949, the second prototype flew, followed by the third in August of that same year.

Deliveries of the new fighter began in May 1951, and 224 J 29As were produced between 1951 and 1953. Next in line was the J 29B, which had increased fuel capacity. In two years, 361 Bs were built. In May 1954, a J 29B beat the previous world speed record held by the American F-86 by 27 km/h. Between 1951 and 1956, 661 Saab J 29s were delivered, and by the end of 1963, all J 29Fs were modified to carry two Sidewinder missiles.

The J 29 was also the first Saab aircraft to see combat. When the Republic of Congo was proclaimed in 1960, the province of Katanga resisted and war broke out. The Congo requested military assistance from the UN, and shortly after, the UN decided to add combat aircraft. Eleven J 29s took part in the operation in which their primary mission was air defense and close support of ground forces.

The service life of the J 29 came to an end in 1972 in the hands of the Austrian Air Force. The Swedish Air Force retired the J 29 from front-line service in May 1967. As Europe's first swept-wing fighter, the J 29 would spend its last days in the less glamorous role as a target tug until 1976.

Though he considered it an ugly duckling on the ground,
British test pilot R.A. "Bob" Moore thought the J 29 a swift once airborne.

PILOT'S PERSPECTIVE
Per Pellebergs
Former Chief Test Pilot for Saab

The J 29 Tunnan was my first fighter aircraft. I finished my training at the Swedish Military Flying School in 1957 and during my time there I flew the Saab Safir and the Vampire.

Moving from the Vampire cockpit onto the J 29, one noticed the many obvious differences between the two aircraft. The cockpit in the J 29 was very roomy, plus it was situated high off the ground. The other big difference was in the number of controls and instruments that were not related to flying the aircraft. There were a number of new instruments and controls dedicated to the navigations and weapons systems. It was a very different aircraft and quite advanced when compared to the cramped Vampire. It was also a hot fighter and not all that easy to fly.

For its day, the cockpit was very comfortable. The parachute was not attached to the seat, so you had to carry your back parachute into the aircraft. It also had two entirely new gadgets in the cockpit. The first was the seemingly very large gunsight and the other was the electronic attitude indicator. Instead of the old mechanical indicator, it was replaced by an electronic beam.

The J 29 did not have a very good heating system, and during winter flying we used fur-lined flights suits and boots. The visibility from the cockpit was absolutely fine. The workload in the cockpit was also very light. During an intercept mission, we would be vectored to a target with the help of ground-based radar, and once we were close enough, it was up to us to find the target. After a while we became very familiar with the aircraft, and the J 29 gave very good aerodynamic indications when approaching a stall or when pulling too many Gs. This meant you could keep your head up and out of the cockpit.

Compared to the Vampire, the J 29 was a very sensitive aircraft to fly and it took a couple of flights to get use to it. Especially the boosted ailerons took some time to get used to. I flew the J 29 from 1957 until 1962.

SAAB J 29B TUNNAN
Flygvapenmuseum, Sweden

1. Landing Gear Down Button
2. Landing Gear Up Button
3. Low Pressure Fuel Handle
4. Engine Fire Extinguisher Button
5. High Pressure Fuel Handle
6. JATO Rockets Release Handle
7. Emergency Air Gauge
8. Outside Air Temp
9. Emergency Landing Gear Down Handle
10. Hydraulic Pressure Gauge
11. Gyro Compass Selector
12. Compass Light Switch
13. Spare Compass
14. Gunsight
15. Accelerometer
16. Main Power Switch
17. Map Holder
18. Climb Indicator
19. Airspeed Indicator
20. Cockpit Light
21. Altimeter
22. Artificial Horizon
23. Gyro Compass
24. Artificial Horizon Release Button
25. Gyro Free Indicator
26. Gyro Locked Indicator
27. Artificial Horizon Lock Button
28. Fuel Gauge
29. Turn-and-Bank Indicator
30. Direction Indicator
31. Fuel Quantity Selector Switch
32. Fuel Warning Light
33. Aft Ball Bearing Thermometer
34. Rudder Pedal Adjustment Handle
35. Nose Steering Wheel
36. Switch Tail Adjusting Gear
37. Control Switch
38. Gun Button
39. Gun Button Safety
40. Cockpit Pressure Gauge

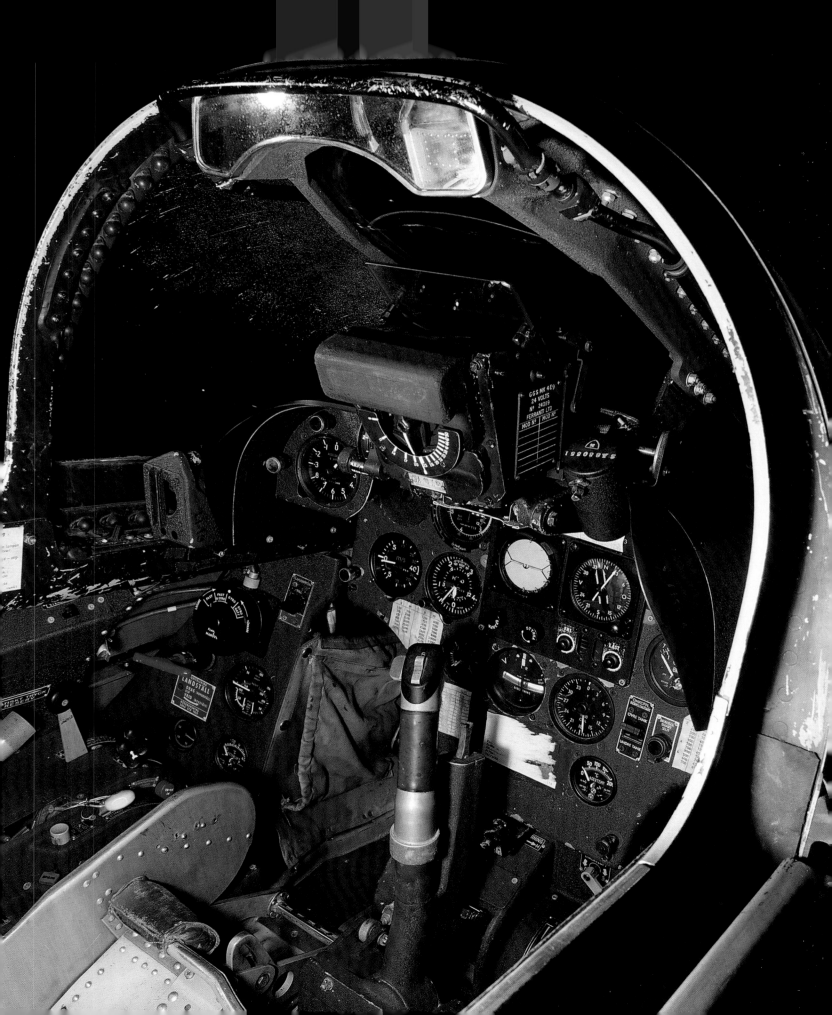

SAAB

J 32 LANSEN

THE AIR FORCE DEMANDS WERE SIMPLE: BUILT A FIGHTER-BOMBER
CAPABLE OF ATTACKING TARGETS ALONG SWEDEN'S 1,245-MILE (2,000 KM) COASTLINE
IN LESS THAN ONE HOUR, IN ALL KINDS OF WEATHER, ALL FROM A CENTRAL BASE.

Aeronautical development in the late 1940s was moving at rapid pace. Equally impressive were the dramatic discoveries in the electronic and radar systems designed for airborne use. In the early 1950s, the Swedish Air Force called for a replacement for existing attack, reconnaissance and night-fighter aircraft. On November 3, 1952, the Avon-powered prototype of the J 32 Lansen took to the air. Three additional aircraft were also ordered. The J 32 proved another first for Saab. It was the first two-seat Swedish jet fighter with a built-in search radar.

Armed with four 20 mm cannon and capable of carrying bombs, rockets and missiles, the J 32 was a true systems aircraft. On March 25, 1953, a Lansen exceeded the speed of sound while in a shallow dive. Production aircraft were powered by a Flygmotor RM 5A (license-built Avon RA 7 engine) of 7,630-pound (3,460 kg) thrust with afterburner. The A 32A attack version of the fighter was capable of carrying four 550-pound (250 kg) bombs, twenty-four 5.7-inch (14.5 cm) rockets, twelve 7-inch (18 cm) rockets, twelve 242-pound (100 kg) bombs, or two Rb 04 anti-ship missiles. There were 287 A 32As produced and, between December 1955 and 1957, these served in all five attack wings of the Swedish Air Force.

The next version of the J 32 produced was the C reconnaissance version. The built-in nose cannons were removed and replaced with a battery of cameras. Forty-four S-32Cs were delivered.

In 1955, development of an all-weather fighter version began. The J 32B made it first flight in January 1957, with 50 percent more engine power. The armament was also increased, from four 20 mm cannons to four 30 mm with a higher rate of fire and a muzzle power three and a half times greater than the 20 mm Hispano guns. Four Sidewinder missiles could also be carried. The J 32B was a truly formidable fighter in both the air-to-air and the attack mission profile. One of the reasons was the new S6A sighting systems, which could display targets in darkness and bad weather. The S6A system also worked with the new radar-sighting system, plus an infrared camera mounted under the wing could illuminate targets at night and in all weather conditions. It was probably the first time a European fighter could engage targets beyond visual range (BVR). The new Saab was also equipped with auto-pilot, which made the aircraft a very stable weapons platform and eased the pilot's work load.

In total, including two prototypes, 120 J 32Bs were delivered between 1958 and 1960. In the early 1970s, twenty-four aircraft were transferred to the Target Flying Squadron at Mamslatt. Four aircraft were modified as target tugs and twelve were turned into electronic countermeasures trainers. Three J 32s are on the civilian register and being used by Sevnsk Flygtjanst for target operations.

During its seven-year production, a total of 449 Lansens and seven prototypes were built. It was, at the time, the equal to and in many cases better than anything the British or Americans had in service. This innovative trend would continue with the Draken and Viggen.

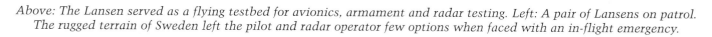

Above: The Lansen served as a flying testbed for avionics, armament and radar testing. Left: A pair of Lansens on patrol. The rugged terrain of Sweden left the pilot and radar operator few options when faced with an in-flight emergency.

PILOT'S PERSPECTIVE
Squadron Leader Tore Eriksson
Swedish Air Force (Ret.)

I first flew the S 32C (reconnaissance version) in 1958. Before that I flew the reconnaissance version of the J 29, the S 29. My total time in the S 32C amounted to 650 hours and I was a squadron leader flying the S 32C from 1969 to 1974.

When I first sat in the S 32C, the first thing I noticed was how comfortable it was. The cockpit was bigger than the S 29 and you had more room to move around. The environmental controls were very good, and the instruments and controls were close to hand and easy to reach. Visibility was excellent from the S 32C. The only time your view was somewhat restricted was when you had to land. The S 32C had a long nose, so when you came in for a landing you had to look to the side to make sure you were on the right track. Cockpit lighting in the S 32C was also very good. We flew all weather and that could be very, very tough. Our minimums were an 80-meter cloud base and 1.2-kilometer visibility. Of course, we had a navigator in the back seat and that was a big help.

The workload in the S 32C was very light. When it came time to turn the cameras on, all you had to do was flick a couple of switches and that was it. We flew all our reconnaissance missions at low level. When it came time to take activate the cameras we would "pop up" to a higher altitude take the pictures we had to take and then it was back down to low level. When we flew missions over the Baltic Sea, close to Russian air space, we would fly very low. Of course, if we came too close, Russian fighters would appear to make sure we didn't cross the line. The S 32C was equipped with six cameras. Three were for low-level work, three for high altitude.

The S 32C was a very good aircraft, but it could have used a more powerful engine. You could go supersonic in the S 32C, but that was very rare. You had to go up to 12,000 meters, light the afterburner, and put it into a very steep dive.

SAAB J 32E LANSEN
Flygvapenmuseum, Sweden

1. Side Window Hot Air Handle
2. Landing Gear Down Switch
3. Rudder Trim Switch
4. Wing Flaps Handle
5. Air Brake Handle
6. Emergency Aileron Trim Switch
7. Throttle
8. Windshield Washer Switch
9. Chaff Dispenser Switch
10. Landing Gear Up Button
11. Emergency Canopy Release Handle
12. Radio Control Panel
13. Speed Indicator
14. Ignition Switches
15. Accelerometer
16. F9/5 Indicator
17. Outlet Temp Indicator
18. Amp Meter
19. Stall Warning Light
20. Engine Fire Warning Light
21. Mach Airspeed Indicator
22. Navigation Radar
23. Amp Meter
24. Attitude Indicator
25. Heading Indicator
26. Altimeter
27. Climb Indicator
28. Volt Meter
29. Artificial Horizon
30. Clock
31. Turn-and-Bank Indicator
32. Rudder Pedals
33. Control Stick
34. Ejection Seat Handle
35. Fuel Tank/Hydraulic Warning Lights

The J 32 was a very versatile design and along with being an effective all-weather fighter it also proved itself in the ground attack, anti-shipping, reconnaissance, electronic countermeasures and advanced trainer role.

SAAB

J 35 DRAKEN

THE UNUSUAL, BUT HIGHLY EFFECTIVE "DOUBLE DELTA" LAYOUT OF THE DRAKEN
(THE DRAGON) PRODUCED A SUPERSONIC FIGHTER WITH A PHENOMENAL RATE OF CLIMB
AND AN EXTRAORDINARY SHORT TAKE-OFF AND LANDING CAPABILITY.

The genesis of the Draken began in the autumn of 1949. Studies for a replacement for the J 29 had begun. The requirement was for a fast, high-flying interceptor with a top speed of Mach 1.5. Much hope was held in the use of a delta configuration, but two accidents in the United Kingdom produced a wave of skepticism with regard to the delta platform. But Saab decided to forge ahead and built an experimental aircraft known as the Saab 210. The Saab 210 research aircraft was used to test the very advanced "double delta" wing. The performance of the Saab 210 was limited because it was powered by a small Armstrong Siddeley Adder engine with only 5 to 10 percent of the new fighter's thrust. All 877 of the test flights proved extremely useful.

Encouraged by the test results, the Swedish Air Force ordered three prototypes under the designation J 35 in April 1952. The unique double-delta wing of the Draken was developed to meet both the high-speed and low-speed requirements, and short take-off and landing distances. To achieve this, the inner wing was given 80 degrees of sweep while the outer wing had 60 degrees sweep, providing lift in the lower speed range. The inner wing was a low-drag design, but was broad and thick. This allowed ample space for the air intakes, main under-carriage, fuel and cannon armament. The new double-delta fighter flew for the first time on October 25, 1955. The second and third prototypes quickly followed. On January 26, 1956, the new Draken exceeded Mach 1 in a climb without afterburner.

Delivery of the production version of the J 35A began in late 1959. These aircraft were powered by the Rolls-Royce Avon Series 200 (RM 6B) engine of 10,780-pound (4,890 kg) dry thrust. Armament for the new fighter consisted of two 30 mm Aden-type cannons and four Sidewinder (Rb 24) missiles. The next version to enter service was the J 35B, which was equipped with a greatly improved radar and new collision-course sighting system. This version also exceeded Mach 2 in level flight. Further development produced the J 35D, with an even more powerful engine — 17,200-pound thrust (7,800 kg). The J 35D carried more fuel and improved avionics. A reconnaissance version of the Draken was also produced and designated the S 35E. The final version to see service was the J 35F. The new F was equipped with a host of features, including a new weapons system incorporating the United States Hughes HM 55 and HM 58 Falcon missiles system. The new J 35F became the most advanced fighter of European design and would remain unchallenged for many years to come.

Because of the Draken's unique short take-off and landing characteristics, the Swedish Air Force was able to develop the capability to use specially prepared stretches of highways as temporary bases, thus greatly increasing their survivability. The Draken has also proven itself in the export market: 51 were ordered by the Danes, 12 by the Finns, and 24 refurbished J 35Ds by the Austrians.

The J 35 Draken has only just recently been retired from Swedish service. In all, including the prototypes, 604 Drakens were built.

Left: The Draken's unique double delta wing is clearly illustrated in this picture.
Above: An Austrian Air Force J 35.

PILOT'S PERSPECTIVE
Per Pellebergs
Former Chief Test Pilot for Saab

I transitioned onto the J 35 Draken in 1962. The Draken was built for both high- and low-altitude supersonic flight. The Draken was the first aircraft that combined low speed and short landing and take-off distances with a Mach 2 capability. Cockpit-wise, moving from the J 29 Tunnan to the Draken, the first thing you noticed was how narrow and small it was. Everything was closer in the Draken cockpit. You felt like you were strapped in more tightly, and in some ways we were. There was a fifth strap that went between your legs, and that made you feel more tightly secured than in the J 29 cockpit. One of the things that was a little more difficult to get used to was the tilted seat. In order to increase the G resistance, the seat was tilted back by about 25 degrees. That meant you had a totally different sitting position. The other thing that was new in the Draken cockpit was the vertical tape instruments. The whole idea was to give you a better tactical awareness, and with these new indicators you could see your target's altitude as well as your own. That was a big advantage.

The visibility in the J 35 was totally different from the J 29's. The visibility to the rear was not very good, and because of the high nose-angle when landing, your forward visibility was somewhat restricted.

Flying an intercept mission in the J 35 was a completely new experience. We worked hard to make the J 35 an efficient all-weather fighter for day and night operations. We relied upon a variety of outside sources to guide us to the target. The Draken, of course, was also equipped with its own radar, but before that became effective, we were directed to the target by a new data-link intercept system. A little ping in your earphones would indicate that new information was coming in, and then one of the indicators would say "accelerate" or "target altitude" or other tactical info. We also had new weapons with which to shoot down a possible intruder. In the beginning we had unguided rocket pods for air-to-air use, and then later we were equipped the more advanced Sidewinder and Falcon guided missiles.

I flew the J 35 Draken from 1962 until the introduction of the new Viggen.

SAAB J 35F DRAKEN
Flygvapenmuseum, Sweden

1. Emergency Trim Switch
2. Canopy Release Switch
3. Throttle Control
4. Canopy Handle
5. Radar Control Handle
6. Ejection Seat Handle
7. Missile Signal Volume Control
8. Air Brakes Control Switch
9. Radio Control Panel
10. Altitude Warning Light
11. Spare Altimeter
12. Spare Airspeed Indicator
13. Angle-of-Attack Indicator
14. Altimeter
15. Main Power Switch
16. Air Brake Indicator
17. Gunsight
18. Mach Airspeed Indicator
19. Turn-and-Bank Indicator
20. Trigger Safety Lock
21. Elevator Trim
22. Auto-pilot Off Button
23. Radio Transmission Button
24. Control Stick
25. Radar
26. Heading Indicator
27. Course Setting Device
28. Artificial Horizon
29. Speed Indicator
30. Distance Altitude Command Indicator
31. Altitude Pressure Setting
32. Outlet Temperature Indicator
33. Fuel Contents Gauge

The export version of the Draken J 35F was the Saab 35XS, seen here in the colors of the Finnish Air Force.

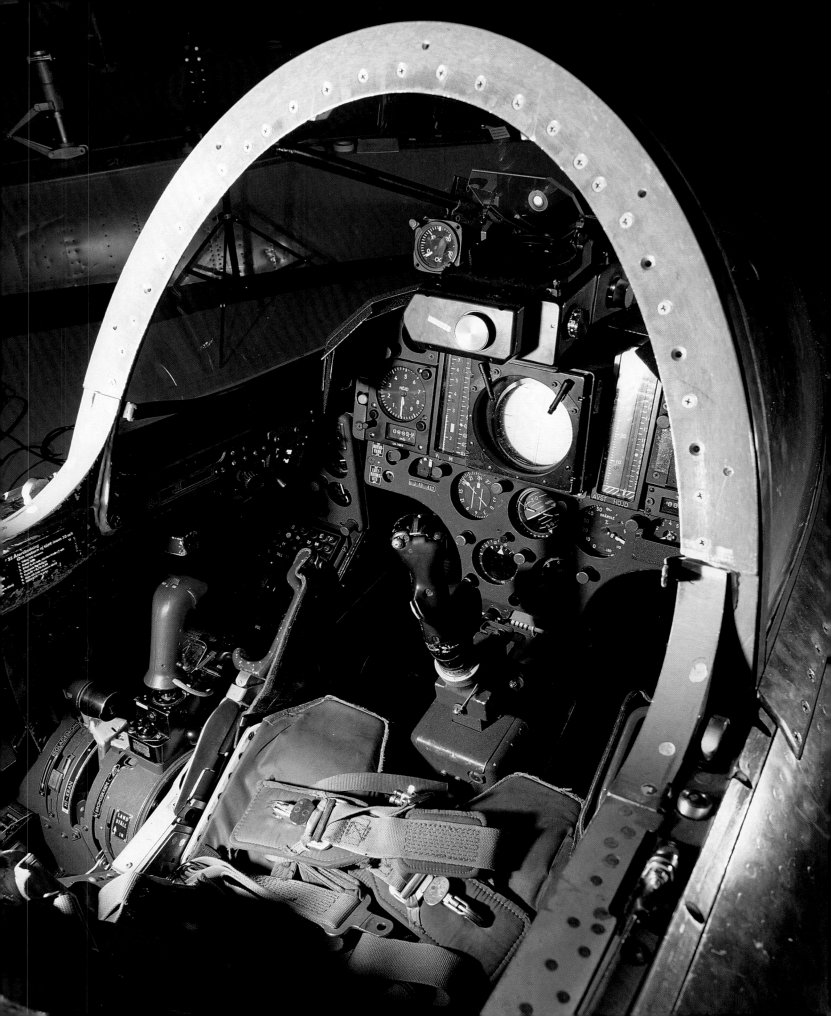

RUSSIA

MIKOYAN MiG-15   MIKOYAN MiG-21   SUKHOI SU-7   MIKOYAN MiG-23

MiG-15

SIMPLE AND TOUGH, THE MiG-15 EARNED THE NAME SAMOLYOT SOLDAT (SOLDIER AEROPLANE).
DESIGNED TO DEFEND RUSSIAN CITIES FROM HIGH-ALTITUDE BOMBERS, THE MiG-15
WOULD SOON FIGHT A VERY DIFFERENT WAR ABOVE THE YALU RIVER.

On Sunday, June 25, 1950, hundreds of tanks and 90,000 men of the North Korean Army plunged into South Korea. Amid squalls of rain, 150 prop-driven combat aircraft swept ahead of the ground troops, causing panic and confusion among the defending South Koreans. Five days later, U.S. ground troops were committed to the defense of Korea, and Air Force units were given free rein to attack targets on the entire Korean peninsula. American fighter response in those first days consisted of piston-engine F-82 twin Mustangs and F-80 Shooting Stars (America' first operational jet). Against the piston-engine Lavochkin La-7s, Yak-3s, 7s, 9s and 18s, the American were clearly superior. By the end of July, the Allies had

complete air superiority over the battlefield, but that was about to change.

On November 1, 1950, six of the world's most advanced fighters made their combat debut. From across the Yalu River, which separated China and North Korea, they rose and made their way south. Helmed by Soviet pilots, they soon found a group of F-51D Mustangs and attacked. First flown on December 30, 1947, just ninety days after the F-86, the new swept-wing fighter was powered by a RD-45F turbojet, a copy of the Rolls-Royce Nene engine. Armed with one 37 mm cannon and two 23 mm cannons, the new MiG-15 boasted a speed of 640 mph at 10,000 feet (1,030 km/h at 3,050 m). No one in the

This MiG-15 is the aircraft flown to South Korea on September 21, 1953, by Lieutenant Kim Sok No (now Kenneth Rowe, see Pilot's Perspective on page 168). It was test flown by five Air Force pilots, including Chuck Yeager. The cockpit of this aircraft appears on page 169.

West knew much about the new MiG, and it quickly proved its superiority over the F-80, F-84, Gloster Meteor, F9F Panther and F2H Banshee — all straight-winged fighters. By the end of November 1950, UN Forces found themselves facing 50 Chinese divisions and about 400 MiG-15s. To meet the new threat, F86A Sabres of the 4th Fighter Interceptor Wing were rushed to Korea.

While the MiG-15 was the world's best interceptor at the time, its lack of bomb-carrying ability restricted its use to purely fighter operations. Had the new fighter been used in the ground-attack role, the Korean War would have been different. As it turned out, the MiG-15 was limited to an area just south of the Yalu River — known as MiG Alley. On paper, the MiG-15 and F-86 were closely matched. While the MiG-15 was lighter than the F-86 with a better rate of climb, a higher ceiling, better acceleration and better turning ability above 30,000 feet, both types had comparable rates of turn between 25,000 and 30,000 feet. While the MiG-15 was more heavily armed, its three cannons were more suited for attacking bombers than fighters. It also suffered from a primitive gunsight that often failed during high-G maneuvering. The F-86, with its six .50-caliber machine guns, created a buzz-saw cone of fire with a greater chance of more rounds hitting the target. The MiG-15 held an advantage over the F-86, however, it became clear that pilot quality and attitude gave the F-86 a clear edge (many were veterans of the Second World War). Soviet practice was to rotate large numbers of pilots, often after completing just forty sorties. This meant hard-won lessons were not passed on to the new men in the front line. The U.S. Air Force also employed better tactics, and Sabre units were able to match their tactics with their aircraft's performance.

In the end, as good as it was, the MiG-15 was not exploited to its full potential. The USAF lost 971 aircraft, and the Navy and Marine Corps 1033, but fewer than 10 percent were actually shot down in air-to-air combat. The MiG-15 was one of the most successful fighters of the Cold War and was built in greater numbers than any other jet fighter. A remarkable 16,000-plus MiG-15s were produced.

PILOT'S PERSPECTIVE
Kenneth Rowe
Formerly Lt. Kim Sok No, NKAF

I first flew the MiG-15 in the spring of 1951. During the Korean War, I flew with the 60th Fighter Squadron of the NKAF with over 100 combat missions.

The controls and instruments in the MiG-15 cockpit were easy to reach and close to hand. The control stick was longer than the F-86's, due to the lack of hydraulic systems for the flight-control surfaces, so it had to be long to utilize the mechanical advantage. The later model MiG-15 bis had a hydraulic system for controlling the ailerons only, not the elevator. The cockpit was cramped for a person over 200 pounds. The environmental controls for maintaining standard atmospheric pressure did not function well. The cockpit pressure at 50,000 feet was about a half of the standard atmospheric pressure at sea level. The cockpit temperature was nearly freezing above 36,000 feet and about 100 degrees Fahrenheit at low altitude on hot summer days. Visibility was not as good as the F-86's, and the MiG's double cockpit plate glass was not as transparent as the F-86's.

During operational sorties I found the control stick heavy at low altitudes and the general performance poor. The cannon shells, loaded in the nose, increased the nose weight, so the plane was hard to pull up from a steep dive.

Originally, the 37 mm and 23 mm cannons were wired to fire separately. Soon after the MiG-15 entered the Korean War, it was rewired to fire all three cannons with a single trigger. The MiG-15 was designed to shoot down large bombers rather than engage in air-to-air dogfighting. The MiGs did accomplish the task of stopping the daylight bombing raids by B-29s, but when the F-86 appeared in MiG Alley, the MiGs had no choice but to engage. The MiG-15's rate of fire was slower than the F-86's six 12.7 mm machine guns. Many MiG-15s kept flying even after being hit by many machine-gun shells because of the MiG's minimal hydraulic system. The F-86 could turn sharply at low altitudes with a smaller radius than the MiG-15, but the MiG's thrust-to-weight ratio was greater, therefore, the MiG could climb faster with a higher ceiling of over 50,000 feet.

If I could have changed anything in the MiG-15 cockpit, it would have been to improve the environmental controls and the hydraulic control systems for the ailerons and elevator.

MIKOYAN MiG-15 BIS
USAF Museum, Dayton, Ohio

1. Canopy Lock
2. Accelerometer
3. Cabin Light Switches
4. Canopy Release Lock
5. Airspeed Indicator
6. Ultra-violet Light
7. Altimeter
8. Oxygen Pressure
9. Mach Meter
10. Artificial Horizon
11. Clock
12. Brake Lever
13. Gunsight
14. Rate-of-Climb Indicator
15. Gyro Compass
16. Oil and Fuel Temp Gauge
17. Control Column
18. Course Indicator
19. Fuel Indicator
20. Voltmeter
21. Ultra Violet Light
22. Fuel Pressure
23. Starboard Electric's Panel
24. Emergency Undercarriage Release
25. Canopy Jettison
26. Emergency Flap Release
27. Homing-Beam Control
28. Ejector Seat Handgrip

MiG-21

DESCRIBED AS A FIGHTER THAT GOES NOWHERE AND DOES NOTHING, THE EXTRAORDINARILY SUCCESSFUL MiG-21 REMAINS THE MOST WIDELY USED COLD WAR FIGHTER IN THE WORLD.

The MiG-21 was the Soviet Union's first production fighter capable of Mach 2 in level flight and is one of the most controversial warplanes of the 1960s, 1970s and 1980s.

Designed as a clear-weather, point-defense air-superiority fighter, the small-tailed delta-wing MiG-21 remains a subject of great contention. Small and lightweight, the MiG-21 has been criticized for its lack of useful armament, poor avionics, engine response and radius of action. However, the MiG-21 is very maneuverable, has excellent short-field performance and is simple to service and maintain. Early versions were described simply as "supersonic sports planes," but progressive improvements have made the MiG-21 the most cost-effective Mach 2 air-superiority fighter in the world.

Born out of the experiences of the Korean War, where the MiG-15 suffered at the hands of the more well trained USAF F-86 pilots, the MiG-21 would emerge as a fast-climbing, short-range interceptor armed with two 30 mm cannons (one cannon was later removed to save weight) and two K-13 (Atoll) infrared homing air-to-air missiles. In early 1956, the first prototype MiG-21 took to the air. In the last quarter of 1959, the Soviet Air Force began to receive their new fighter.

Designated the MiG-21F, the new fighter was only good for fair-weather operations. Its single 30 mm cannon, simple radar and K-13A missiles (considered unsatisfactory for anything but docile targets in clear weather) were obviously inadequate for the job. But what it lacked in armament and potency, the MiG-21

Above right: A Soviet pilot climbs aboard his MiG-21.
Below: A Polish Navy MiG-21 at low level.

more than made up for in maneuverability, excellent handling characteristics, good visibility and simple servicing and maintenance. Throughout the 1960s the MiG-21 was progressively improved, but the constant Achilles heel for the MiG-21 remained fuel. The internal fuel capacity of 638 gallons (2,900 L) was distributed between seven self-sealing tanks, and even with the addition of a 108-gallon (490 L) centerline drop tank, the MiG's effective cruise endurance is still only about an hour.

Despite this, the MiG-21's performance and all-round simplicity resulted in its adoption by no fewer than fifty-six air forces around the world! During the Vietnam War, the Vietnamese People's Air Force produced thirteen MiG-21 aces. Considered equal to the F-4 Phantom and F-8 Crusader in maneuverability and acceleration, the MiG-21 proved a formidable foe against the more sophisticated American fighters. Taking advantage of the MiG's light weight, the North Vietnamese were able to airlift individual aircraft to auxiliary airfields. From these airfields and using strap-on solid-fuel rocket boosters, the MiGs were able to mount surprise attacks on incoming American raids. Using this technique, North Vietnamese pilots were able to pop up from nowhere, quickly engage the enemy and return to a conventional base.

To date the MiG-21 has seen action in at least thirty shooting wars, as recently as the Gulf War and in Yugoslavia in the summer of 1991. Total production of the MiG-21, including foreign manufacture, stands at 13,500. No other Western Cold War fighter comes close. The MiG-21 still flies today and, with companies such as Israel Aircraft Industries specializing in MiG-21 upgrades, the go-nowhere, do-nothing fighter will continue to fly for years to come.

PILOT'S PERSPECTIVE
Squadron Leader Lieutenant Commander Slawek Olczyk
Polish Navy (Ret.)

I first flew the MiG-21 bis in May 1992. I graduated from aviation school in 1987 and started to fly the MiG-15 and MiG-17, which I flew for five years. I also flew the Tornado three times. In total, I have 1,282 hours flying the MiG-17 and 21.

When I moved from the MiG-17 to the MiG-21, I thought the 21 cockpit was fantastic, but my enthusiasm soon disappeared. In the MiG-17 the cockpit was equipped with manual indicators and buttons. There were no electronic instruments. The MiG-21 cockpit was also equipped with manual indicators and, while not that comfortable, it was bigger and the ejection seat was much better and safer. It was very narrow and there was no place to rest your hands or your arms. The visibility was also extremely limited. The seat was set very deep in the cockpit, and you couldn't raise it to a suitable level. When you compared it to the F-16, there was no contest.

The environmental controls in the cockpit had to be set before flight. You could not change them once you were airborne. You had three temperatures to choose from: 20 degrees, 25 degrees, or 16 degrees Celsius.

During an intercept mission, the workload in the cockpit could be very heavy. While flying the aircraft, you had to operate radar, select and activate your weapons, and manage your fuel. Our radar had maximum range of 15 kilometers. The manual said it was 30, but that was only on the newest aircraft.

Compared to the Tornado, the MiG-21 is faster, but much more sensitive. Just a small movement of the stick would cause the aircraft to move. Engine response is not instantaneous. There is three to five seconds delay before the engine actually powers up after you move the throttle. This was a problem when you flew in large formations.

If I could have changed anything in the MiG-21 cockpit, it would have been the weapons controls. There were too many buttons and they were scattered around the cockpit. You had to actually switch hands while flying to activate some of the controls.

MIKOYAN MiG-21F
USAF Museum, Dayton, Ohio

1. Oxygen Install Switch
2. Rocket/Cannon Arming Switch
3. Flap Switches
4. Seat Control Switch
5. Navigation Lights Switch
6. Throttle
7. Air Start Switch
8. Anti-Surge Valves Switch
9. Emergency Nozzle Control
10. Hydraulic Pump Switches
11. K-18 Oxygen Gauge
12. Landing Gear Lever
13. Landing Gear Position Indicator
14. UD-1 Range Indicator
15. Break and Overload Warning Lights
16. V-1 Voltmeter
17. Accelerometer
18. Landing Light Switch
19. External Tank Drop Switch
20. ARU-37 Automatic Control
21. Airspeed Indicator
22. Compass
23. Radio Switch
24. Trim Control
25. Gun/Radar Sight
26. Attitude Indicator
27. Altimeter
28. Clock
29. Cannon Indicator Lights
30. Rate-of-Climb Indicator
31. Landing Gear Warning Light
32. Trim/Stabilizer Warning Lights
33. Emergency Pitot Tube Switches
34. Cockpit Pressure Gauge
35. Turn-and-Bank Indicator
36. Oil Pressure Indicator
37. Missile Control Panel
38. Mach Meter
39. Tachometer
40. Exhaust Temp Gauge
41. Fuel Tank Pump Switches
42. Fuel Flowmeter
43. Control Stick
44. M-2000 Pressure Gauge
45. Wheels Pressure Gauge
46. Fuses

A MiG-21 in Finnish colors. The Finnish Air Force took delivery of their first MiG-21Fs in 1963.

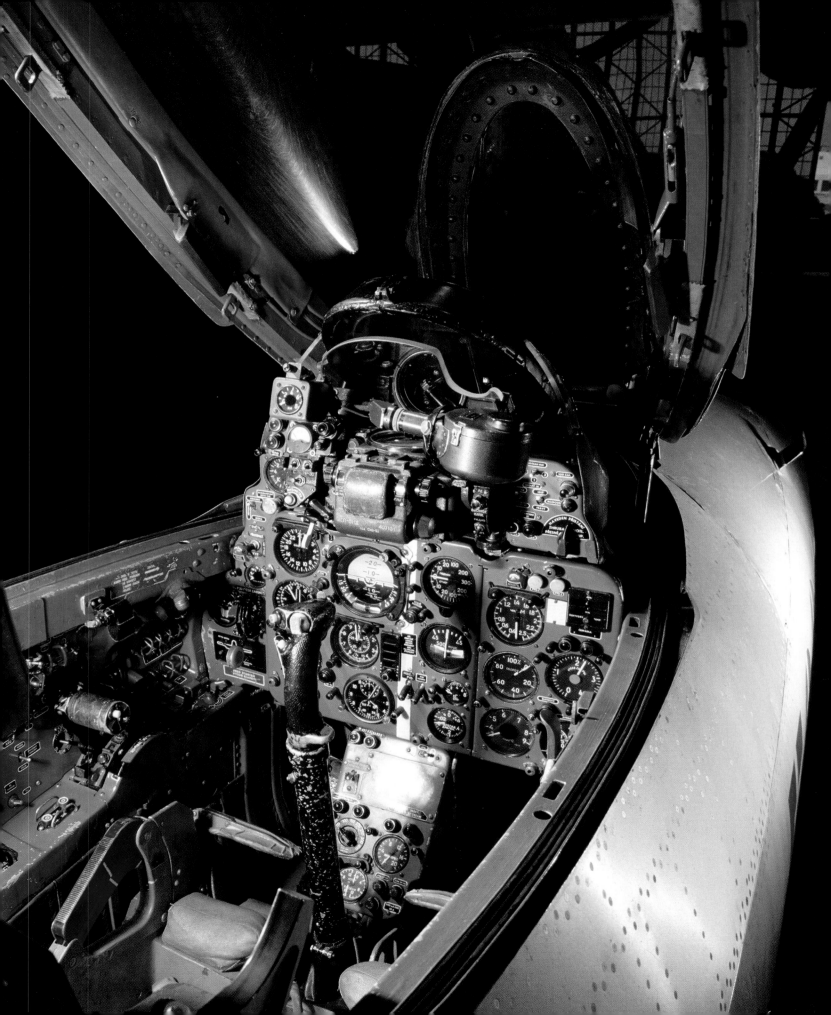

SUKHOI

SU-7

OFTEN OVERSHADOWED BY THE MIG SERIES OF FIGHTERS, THE SUKHOI SU-7, IN ITS NUMEROUS VERSIONS, HAS PROVEN TO BE ONE OF THE MOST SUCCESSFUL FIGHTERS EVER BUILT IN THE SOVIET UNION.

The Sukhoi series of fighters is a fine example of the Russian method of taking a proven aircraft and continually upgrading it over a long period of time. From the Sukhoi S-1 prototype came the Su-7 ground-attack fighter, the Su-9 interceptor, the Su-17/20/22 variable-wing fighter-bomber and the Su-15 interceptor. All these aircraft shared common airframe components, and for over thirty years they contributed to more than half of all tactical ground-attack fighter regiments in the Soviet Union and Warsaw Pact.

By the end of the Second World War, the Sukhoi Design Bureau, led by Pavel Ossipovich Sukhoi, had built a number of promising fighter and ground-attack prototypes, but none of these aircraft ever reached production status. In 1949, the entire Soviet aviation industry was reorganized. The Sukhoi Design Bureau was disbanded and the Sukhoi's staff was returned to the Tupolev OKB. With the death of Joseph Stalin in 1953, Sukhoi was allowed to reform his own design bureau. Almost immediately Sukhoi and his staff began work on the Sukhoi S-1 prototype. The new S-1 was equipped with a 62-degree swept-back wing and was powered by a single AL-7 turbojet engine of 14,300 pounds (6,490 kg) thrust. The first flight of the S-1 prototype in September 1955 proved highly successful, and in 1956 the new fighter achieved Mach 2.

In 1957, the Soviet Air Force selected the MiG-21 as its primary interceptor and chose the Sukhoi design to fill the ground-attack role. Work on modifying the S-1 soon followed, and the first prototype, designated S-22, flew for the first time in April 1957. No internal armament was carried, but the S-22 was equipped for four pylons. After numerous modifications, including a new SRD-5 radar and modified wing, the S-22 was ordered into production under the designation Sukhoi Su-7 (NATO codename Fitter).

The first production Su-7s entered the Soviet Frontal Aviation Units in 1958. The new Su-7Bs (B for Bombardardirovshckik, fighter-bomber) were armed with two 30 mm NR-30 cannons, which had the ability to penetrate the rear armor of a main battle-tank, including the American M-60. Because the Su-7's internal fuel capacity was only 646 gallons (2,445 L) and the AL-7 turbojet consumed fuel at a prodigious rate, especially at low levels, the Su-7 was equipped with a pair of 158-gallon (600 L) drop tanks. This reduced the weapons load to just 2,200 pounds (1,000 kg). Without the drop tanks, the Su-7's range was a meager 155 miles. But despite these shortcomings, the Su-7 has proven to be a very reliable and stable gun platform, particularly in the low-level regime, and with its generous flap area and wide-track landing gear, the Su-7 can also operate from rough, unprepared airfields.

In 1968, the Su-7 saw combat during the India-Pakistan War and then again with the Egyptian Air Force in several of the Arab-Israeli Wars. The Su-7's handling qualities and speed at low level were praised by both Indian and Egyptian pilots. The only criticism was the Su-7's vulnerability to small-caliber anti-aircraft fire.

The Su-7 series fighters were widely exported and served successfully in the air forces of Afghanistan, Cuba, Czechoslovakia, Egypt, India, Poland, Syria and Vietnam.

Right: The Su-7 was considered a "heavy fighter" in the same category as the F-105.
Capable of supersonic speeds at low level, the Su-7 posed a serious threat to NATO.

PILOT'S PERSPECTIVE
Major Boguslaw Zych
Polish Air Force

I first flew the Su-7 in April 1988 with the 3rd Fighter Bomber Regiment of the Polish Air Force. Previous to that I flew the TS-11 Iskra, the SBLim-2 (Polish-built MiG-15UTI) and Lim-5 (Polish-built MiG-17) during my training at the Polish Air Force Academy. I have a total of 100 hours on the Su-7. From there I moved onto the Su-22, and since 1989 I have accumulated a total of 1,550 hours on both types.

When I first sat in the Su-7 cockpit, I was overwhelmed by the number of instruments and switches — over 200! I thought to myself, I will have to be a Mozart or a virtuoso to fly this thing!

The Su-7 is a very large aircraft and the cockpit is the same but very comfortable. The air conditioning is very simple and we couldn't change the temperature during flight. The cockpit had no ergonomic sense to it at all, but the instruments and controls are within easy reach. Visibility from the Su-7 cockpit was extremely poor, and when landing the aircraft, you could not see the wings from the cockpit. And because of the high landing speeds (450–420 km/h) many young pilots found the Su-7 a very difficult aircraft to land, especially in bad weather. The Su-7 was not equipped with ILS (instrument landing system) or TACAN (tactical air navigation). You didn't have time to make a mistake!

If I could have changed anything in the Su-7 cockpit, it would have been the ejection seat. Pilots who ejected usually injured their backs. I would have also added an angle-of-attack instrument (especially during aerobatics) as well as an improved gunsight and a modern nav/attack system.

SUKHOI SU-7BKL
Polish Aviation Museum, Krakow, Poland

1. Emergency Braking Handle
2. Cone Position Switches
3. Intake Diffuser System Steering
4. Engine Start Switches
5. In-Flight Engine Start-Up Switch
6. Brake Chute Release
7. Underwing Stores Emergency Drop Switches
8. Control Stick Load Setting Switch
9. Front Wheel Steering
10. Brake Chute Lock Open Indicator
11. Heating Switches
12. Landing Lights Switch
13. RATO Engine Automatic Start Switch

14. RATO Engines Manual Drop Switch
15. Fast Heating Switch
16. Cockpit Pressure Gauge
17. Landing Gear Lever
18. Afterburner Emergency Switches
19. Gun/Radar Sight
20. G-Force Indicator
21. Oil Pressure Gauge
22. Landing Gear Position Indicator
23. Emergency Landing Gear Down Handle
24. Airspeed Indicator
25. Altimeter
26. Control Stick
27. Trim Switch
28. Gyro Compass
29. Oil Pressure Gauge
30. Tubes Pressure Gauge

31. Instrument Illumination Control
32. Gyro Compass Lock Switch
33. Off Course Warning Light
34. Course Indicator
35. Voltmeter
36. Fuel Pressure Gauge
37. Range Finder Switches
38. Instrument Illumination Control
39. Turn-and-Bank Indicator
40. Engine RPM Drop Indicator
41. Tachometer
42. Automatic Generator Feed Switch and Indicator
43. Mach Meter
44. Engine Status Indicators
45. Exhaust Gas Temp Gauge

The Su-7's internal fuel capacity seriously affected its combat radius. This Polish Su-7 is equipped with four drop tanks on both the fuselage and wing pylons.

MIKOYAN
MiG-23

COMBINING A NASA-STYLE OUTBOARD-HINGED WING WITH
PHANTOM-TYPE MULTI-SHOCK LATERAL INTAKES, THE MiG-23 PROVED
THE MOST IMPORTANT SOVIET FIGHTER OF THE MID-1960S TO EARLY 1970S.

The development of the MiG-23 dates back to the late 1950s and early 1960s. The threat of tactical nuclear weapons called for aircraft with good short-field performance. The idea was that, in case of emergency, aircraft could be moved to auxiliary airfields and thus saved from destruction. The new fighter was also designed to replace the nimble MiG-21 and become an effective multi-role aircraft.

In an effort to improve short-field performance, the MiG design team decided to develop two different prototypes in parallel. One had a swing-wing design, and the other was the MiG-23DPD, which incorporated a delta wing with two forward-inclined lift engines and a single turbojet engine.

The lift engines were mounted in an engine bay in the center of the fuselage. The MiG-23DPD flew for the first time in April 1967, in competition with the MiG-23I, the swing-wing prototype. The MiG-23I had a clear advantage over the MiG-23DPD. The three engines in the MiG-23DPD reduced the aircraft's internal fuel capacity and it used large quantities of fuel just taking off and landing. The MiG-23DPD was dropped, and all energy was focused on the swing-wing MiG-23I.

The swing-wing design on the MiG-23 showed a remarkable resemblance to that of the American F-111. Whether the Soviets merely copied the American design is not clear. The advantages of the swing wing were many. When fully spread, the swing wing offered excellent short take-off and landing performance

while carrying a heavy weapons load. In the fully swept position, a high top speed and good super-sonic handling could be maintained. The MiG-23I prototype flew for the first time in April 1967, and it was ordered into production in 1969.

The new MiG-23 was a big fighter. It had twice the engine thrust of the MiG-21, twice the internal fuel load and gross weight. The first production batch of 100 aircraft were designated MiG-23S and code-named "Flogger" by NATO. These were followed by the slightly improved MiG-23SM and quickly superseded by the more-powerful MiG-23MS Flogger Es. The MS version was equipped with the 22,485-pound-thrust (49,470 kg) Tumansky R-27-300 turbojet. This engine proved more fuel efficient and did not emit the smoke trail that was common with the previous Lyulka engine. A small batch of MiG-23MS Floggers was exported to Algeria, Egypt, Libya, Syria and Iraq.

During the 1982 war in Lebanon, Syrian MiG-23MS fighters entered combat for the first time against the Israeli F-16s. Within a week the Syrians had lost thirty-six Floggers while the Israelis had lost just two aircraft.

In January 1989, Floggers were once again pitted against American-built fighters. Two Libyan MiG-23s were vectored against two F-14 Tomcats from the aircraft carrier USS *John F. Kennedy*. Both Floggers were declared hostile and quickly shot down.

The MiG-23/27 Flogger series of aircraft saw extensive service with the former Soviet Union and its Warsaw Pact allies, including Poland, Hungary, Bulgaria, East Germany, Rumania and Czechoslovakia. Other countries including Libya, Syria, Egypt, India, Cuba, Algeria, Iraq, Afghanistan and North Korea have imported Floggers. It is estimated that more than 4,000 MiG-23/27s have been built.

Above: A Flogger B of the Polish Air Force. Normal armament would consist of four AA-2 Atoll missiles.
Below: The MiG-23, in its many versions, proved itself highly capable in both fighter and ground-attack roles. This Polish MiG-23, with its wings swept back, is configured for high-speed flight.

PILOT'S PERSPECTIVE
Captain Piotr Sitak
Polish Air Force (Ret.)

I flew the MiG-23 for ten years and accumulated 750 hours on the type.

When I graduated from the Air Force Academy, I had a total of 250 hours on the TF-11 jet trainer. Before I soloed in the MiG-23, I had to complete twelve flights in a MiG-23 two-seater. It was an easy aircraft to fly and I was very impressed with both the aircraft and the cockpit. It was a very powerful fighter, with 12,500 kg of thrust and very fast at Mach 2.35.

I would describe the MiG-23 cockpit as comfortable. It was not as big as the Su-17, but for a fighter pilot it was big enough. The controls and instruments were close to hand and easy to reach. In my case, we used the MiG-23 as an interceptor. In that role, everything in the cockpit was well organized, but you could run into a little trouble with the head up display (HUD). The HUD in the MiG-23 displayed only radar and infrared information. The problems started when flying in clouds or toward the sun. It was difficult to read the information. Because you controlled the radar with the HUD, and the flight instruments were in the cockpit, you had to move your eyes from one to the other.

In the interceptor role, the visibility from the MiG-23 was good, but not very good. When it came to dogfighting, I would say it was rather poor. The windshield was too small. It was difficult to see the other aircraft.

The workload in the MiG-23 during an intercept mission was not that heavy. Everything was quite well organized. The MiG-23 was equipped with a one-switch weapons-activation system and a one-switch weapons selector. The only drawback was you had to move your left hand off the throttle in order to turn the weapons selector on.

I cannot find any real fault with the MiG-23 cockpit. I liked it very much. In flight, the environmental controls were no problem, but sometimes it could get too hot on the ground while you taxied.

The ejection seat in the MiG-23 was the same as the MiG-21. It was a good ejection seat but there was one problem. It was not a zero zero seat. You had to be going at least 140 km/h for a successful ejection.

Against the MiG-21, the 23 was the superior fighter because of our radar and our thrust weight rate. But against the MiG-29, it was a totally different situation. There was nothing we could really do against the MiG-29.

MIKOYAN MiG-23MF
Polish Aviation Museum, Krakow, Poland

1. Air Intake Emergency Select Switch
2. Thermo-Regulator Switch
3. Landing Gear Anti-Skid Switch
4. In-Flight Engine Start Switch
5. Brake Chute Release
6. Course Check
7. Canopy Open-Ground Operation
8. Throttle
9. SAU Automatic Pilot Control Panel
10. Landing Lights Control Panel
11. Fire Extinguisher Button
12. Landing Gear Position Indicator
13. Emergency Landing Gear Manual Release
14. Landing Gear Handle
15. SH-13 Armament Selector Panel
16. Nose Wheel Steering In/Out Control
17. Airspeed Indicator
18. Altimeter
19. Mach Meter
20. Control Stick
21. Ejection Handle
22. Angle-of-Attack Indicator
23. G-Meter
24. "Saphir" S-23 Radar Gun Sight
25. Nose Wheel Brake On-Off
26. Artificial Horizon
27. SAU (Automatic Control System) Off Button
28. Trim Button
29. Leveling Off Button
30. Distance Measuring Equipment
31. Armament Selector Switch
32. Primary and Emergency Air Pressure
33. Underwing Armament Switches
34. Turn-and-Bank Indicator
35. Clock
36. Radar Controls
37. Underwing Stores Emergency Drop Switch
38. Tubes Pressure Gauge
39. Air Intake Ramp Position Indicator
40. Wing Position Indicator
41. Course Setting (Automatic/Manual) Switch
42. Oil Pressure Gauge
43. RSBN-6 Control Panel
44. Tachometer
45. Emergency Warning Light Panel
46. Exhaust Gas Temp Gauge
47. Roll Setting Switch
48. LAZUR Control (Data Link) Panel
49. Oxygen Pressure Indicator

"You love a lot of things if you live around them. But there isn't any woman and there isn't any horse, not any before nor any after, that is as lovely as a great airplane. And men who love them are faithful to them even though they leave them for others. Man has one virginity to lose in fighters, and if it is a lovely airplane he loses it to, there is where his heart will forever be."

Ernest Hemingway

Left: Low on fuel and exhausted from the latest combat mission, there's one more dangerous thing this F9F pilot has to do — land his fighter aboard the carrier below.

ACKNOWLEDGMENTS

This book would not have been possible without the help and support of my family and friends. I would also like to thank John Denison, Kathy Fraser and Noel Hudson and everyone at Boston Mills Press and Firefly Books. Thanks to Dan Patterson for his dedication and friendship and to Ron Dick for his insights and generous contributions.

The following people gave their time and expertise to help make this book possible. Grateful thanks to Robert L. Rasmussen, Robert R. Macon, Linda Mason, Natalie Finnigan, Sven Scheiderbaur, Vic Johnston, Urgan Trygg, Phil and Angie Wilkinson, Graham Mottram, Michael Smith, Piotr Lopalewski, Jana Pawla, Jerry Shore, David Morris, Brett Stolle, Wes Henry, Dave Upton, Magnus Karlsson, Mariusz Adamski, William Daysh, Barry Aldous, Hill Goodspeed, Nick Stroud, Richard Norris, Dave MacFarland, Fiona Hale, Andy Ward, to all the pilots who gave so freely of their time and expertise, and to Nick Cosco, photographic Sherpa extraordinaire.

I would also like to thank the following museums: The National Museum of Naval Aviation, Pensacola; the National Aviation Museum, Ottawa; the USAF Museum, Dayton; the RAF Museum, Hendon; the Imperial War Museum, Duxford; the Lightning Preservation Group, Bruntingthorpe; British Aviation Heritage, Bruntingthorpe; the Newark Air Museum, Newark; Flygvapenmuseum, Linkoping; the Fleet Air Arm Museum, Yeovilton; and the Polish Aviation Museum, Krakow.

Dan would like to add special thanks to Cheryl, for her belief, support and tolerance in making the pursuit of these projects possible.

PHOTO CREDITS

Saab: 1, 152, 156, 157, 160, 161, 162
Lockheed: 3, 5, 62, 63, 64
Russell Adams: 96
Ron Dick: 8, 79, 128, 172
Robert F. Dorr: 97
Nick Cosco: 10
Mariusz Adamski: 12, 170
Department of National Defence, Canada: 16, 17, 18, 34, 42, 43, 44, 50, 51
National Museum of Naval Aviation: 23, 46, 78, 82, 83, 86, 87, 90, 91, 182

USAF Museum: 24, 26, 66, 75
National Archives, D.C.: 30, 36, 38, 39, 40, 47, 54, 55, 56, 58, 59, 66, 67, 71, 166, 168, 184
Ministry of Defence, U.K.: 6, 100, 109, 132, 136, 140
Aeroplane Monthly: 101, 105, 106, 124, 125, 126, 129, 146, 147
Fleet Air Arm Museum: 113, 116, 117, 121
Polish Aviation Museum: 175, 176, 178, 179
Andy Leitch: 133

Left: Two F-106s from the 11th Fighter Interceptor Wing, July 1967.

BIBLIOGRAPHY

Andrews, C. F. *Aircraft in Profile Volume 1, Part One.* Birkshire England: Doubleday& Company, 1965.

Andersson, G. Hans. *Saab Aircraft Since 1937.* London: Putnam Aeronautical Books, 1998.

Angelucci, Enzo and Peter Bowers. *The American Fighter: The Definitive Guide to American Fighter Aircraft from 1917 to the Present.* New York: Orion Books, 1985.

Drendel, Lou. *B-52 Stratofortress in Action.* Carrollton, Texas: Squadron/Signal Publications Inc., 1975.

Dick, Ron and Dan Patterson. *American Eagles: A History of the United States Air Force.* Charlottesville, VA: Howell Press, 1997.

Franks, Norman. *Aircraft Versus Aircraft: The Illustrated History Story of Fighter Pilot Combat Since 1914.* New York: Cresent Books, 1990.

Green, William. *The World's Fighting Planes.* London: Macdonald & Co Publishers Ltd., 1964.

Isby, C. David. *Jane's Air War 1: Fighter Combat in the Jet Age.* London: Harper Collins Publishers. 1997.

Jackson, Paul. *Mirage: Modern Combat Aircraft 23.* Surrey, England. Ian Allan Ltd., 1985.

Jarrett Philip. *Putnam's History of Aircraft: The Modern War Machine. Military Aviation Since 1945.* London: Putnam Aeronautical Books, 2000.

Lake, Jon and F. Robert Dorr. *Korean War Aces.* London: Osprey Publishing, 1995.

Lindsay, Roger. *Lightning.* London: Ian Allan Ltd., 1989.

Laming, Tim. *Buccaneer.* Sparkford, Somerset: Haynes Publishing, 1998.

Millberry, Larry. *The Avro CF-100.* Toronto, Canada: CANAV Books, 1981.

Scutts, Jerry. *Fighter Operations.* Somerset, England: Patrick Stephens Ltd., 1992.

Spering, Don and Don Linn. *MiG-21 Fishbed in Action.* Carrollton, Texas: Squadron/Signal Publications Inc., 1993.

Stapfer, Hans-Heiri. *Sukhoi Fitters in Action.* Carrollton, Texas: Squadron/Signal Publications Inc., 1989.

Sullivan, Jim. *AD Skyraider in Action.* Carrollton, Texas: Squadron/Signal Publications Inc., 1983.

Y'Blood, Tom and Lou Drendel. *B-47 Stratojet in Action.* Michigan: Squadron Signal Publications Inc., 1976.

Yefim, Gordon and Bill Gunston. *MiG Aircraft Since 1937.* London: Putnam Aeronautical Books, 1998.

Periodicals

Andrews, C.F. "Fighters of the Fifties Supermarine Scimitar." London: *Aeroplane Monthly*, March 1979.

Andrews, Hal. "Fighters of the Fifties: Grumman Panther." London: *Aeroplane Monthly*, August 1976.

Andrews, Hal. "Fighters of the Fifties: Douglas F4D Skyray." London: *Aeroplane Monthly*, 1977.

Barker, David. "Database Convair B-36 Peacemaker." London: *Aeroplane Monthly*, December 2000.

Braybook, Roy. "MiG-21 Fishbed." London: *Aeroplane Monthly*, June 1975.

Braybrook, Roy. "Lightning." London: *Royal Air Force Year Book*, 1981.

Braybrook, Roy. "Database Hawker Hunter." London: *Aeroplane Monthly*, July 2001.

Burnet, Charles and Eric B. Morgan. "The V-Bombers." London: *Aeroplane Monthly*, August 1980.

Gardner, Brian. "Air Refueling in the RAF." London: *Royal Air Force Yearbook*, 1981.

Gunston, Bill. "Fighters of the Fifties: Avro Canada CF-100." London: *Aeroplane Monthly*, September 1978.

Gunston, Bill. "Fighters of the Fifties: Hawker Hunter." London: *Aeroplane Monthly*, June 1979.

Gunston, Bill. "Fighters of the Fifties: North American F-100 Super Sabre." London: *Aeroplane Monthly*, 1980.

Hukee, Byron. "Down There Amongst Them." Ridgefield, Connecticut: *Flight Journal*, October 1998.

James, Derek. "Database Hawker Sea Hawk." London: *Aeroplane Monthly*, September 2002.

Lindsay, Roger. "Fighters of the Fifties: Gloster Javelin." London: *Aeroplane Monthly*, January 1978.

Turpin, Brian. "Vickers Valiant: The RAF's First V-bomber." London: *Aeroplane Monthly*, February 2002.

Turpin, Brian. "DataBase Vickers Valiant." London: *Aeroplane Monthly*, February 2002

Williams, Ray. "Fighters of Fifties: Hawker Sea Hawk." London: *Aeroplane Monthly*, May 1976.

Wetterhahn, Ralph. "Nguyen Van Bay and the Aces of the North." Washington, D.C.: *Air & Space Smithsonian*, October/November 2000.

Wynn, Humphrey. "The RAF V-Force." London: *Diamond Jubilee Royal Air Force Yearbook*, 1978.

"Five Grand Fighter." London: *Air International*. November 1978.

"Five Grand Fighter: Part Two." London: *Air International*. December 1978.

Aviation News. Volume 4, Number 26. Amersham, England: Alan W. Hall, May 1976.

"Two Decades of the 'Twenty-One'." London: *Air Enthusiast International*. May 1974.

"Mikoyan Fishbed-N." London: *Air International*. December 1979.

"Israel's Pride of Lions." London: *Air International*. November 1976.

"Fighter A to Z." London: *Air International*. May 1977.

"Fighter A to Z." London: *Air International*. April 1977.

INDEX